Core Classics Plus™

Narrative of the Life of Frederick Douglass, an American Slave

by Frederick Douglass

Core Knowledge® Foundation

Core Classics Plus™

Series Editor
Robert D. Shepherd

Editors
Michael L. Ford
Mary Kathryn Hassett
Matthew Davis

What, ho!—our countrymen in chains!

    The whip on *woman's* shrinking flesh!

Our soil still reddening with the stains,

    Caught from her scourging, warm and fresh!

What! mothers from their children riven!

    What! God's own image bought and sold!

Americans to market driven,

    And barter'd as the brute, for gold!

                —*John Greenleaf Whittier*

These lines by the great American poet and abolitionist John Greenleaf Whittier served as the epigraph to the original 1846 edition of Douglass's *Narrative*. They first appeared in William Lloyd Garrison's antislavery newspaper, *The Liberator*.

NARRATIVE OF THE LIFE

OF

FREDERICK DOUGLASS,

AN

AMERICAN SLAVE.

WRITTEN BY HIMSELF.

What, ho!—our countrymen in chains!
  The whip on *woman's* shrinking flesh!
Our soil still reddening with the stains,
  Caught from her scourging, warm and fresh!
What! mothers from their children riven!
  What! God's own image bought and sold!
Americans to market driven,
  And barter'd as the brute, for gold!—*Whittier.*

THIRD ENGLISH EDITION.

WORTLEY, NEAR LEEDS : PRINTED BY JOSEPH BARKER.

1846.

Contents

No. 8.

FREE!

A Note to the Teacher

The Core Knowledge Foundation is pleased to publish this student edition of *Narrative of the Life of Frederick Douglass, an American Slave*. The text is presented in its entirety, as Douglass wrote it, with only occasional editorial emendations, which are clearly indicated in the text itself and explained in the accompanying teacher's guide. Typically, American students encounter Douglass only in the brief selections found in anthologies. This edition has been prepared in the hope that a new generation of young people will have the opportunity to read the entire book, for only extensive exposure to the dramatic and elegant prose of the *Narrative* can enable students to appreciate both the literary power and the life accomplishments that earned Douglass his prominent place in American history.

We suggest that teachers of younger students read the text carefully before assigning it to assess whether their students are ready to encounter its vivid picture of the cruelty of the American slave system. Some teachers might choose to assign selected passages, leaving others for later exploration when students have matured. Chapter 8, which contains Douglass's account of learning to read and write under the most formidable circumstances, should not be missed. The guided reading questions (located in the margins of the text) and the student exercises (located at the ends of chapters) should help teachers to lead young students to an honest and therefore useful encounter with this most tragic period of American history.

All students should find Douglass's devotion to learning and his dedication to human freedom to be a lifelong source of inspiration. They should find, too, in his persuasive and powerful prose a model for their own writing. The questions and exercises are meant to help students translate this reading experience into a deeper understanding of history, a larger working vocabulary, and a greater command of style.

We have moved to the Teacher's Guide two sections of the front matter that appeared in the original edition—the preface by William Lloyd Garrison and the letter from Wendell Phillips. We thought these pieces would provide useful background for the teacher but that their florid nineteenth-century style might be a bit daunting for students. ■

—The Editors

On the Title and Genre of This Work

A narrative is, of course, simply a story. Douglass's work is an example of the literary genre known as the **autobiographical narrative**, or **autobiography**—a work in which a person tells his or her own life story.

The original edition of this book, published in 1846, carried, following the title, the words "Written by Himself." This phrase emphasized the fact that the *Narrative* was one of those works in which someone with real experience of the horrors of slavery had an opportunity to tell the story in his or her own voice.

Douglass's *Narrative* is perhaps the finest example of that subgenre of the autobiography commonly referred to as the **slave narrative.** Other superb slave narratives include the following:

> Olaudah Equiano, *The Interesting Narrative of the Life of Olaudah Equiano, or Gustavus Vassa, the African, Written by Himself* (1789)

> Harriet A. Jacobs, *Incidents in the Life of a Slave Girl, Written by Herself* (1861)

Students may also find of interest the following early African-American narrative:

> Briton Hammon, *Narrative of the Uncommon Sufferings, and Surprising Deliverance of Briton Hammon, a Negro Man, Servant to General Winslow of Marshfield, in New England; Who Returned to Boston, after Having Been Absent Almost Thirteen Years* (1760)

An excellent and extensive collection of narratives by enslaved persons can be found at docsouth.unc.edu/neh/index.html. ■

—The Editors

A Brief Biography of Frederick Douglass[1]

The Early Years

Frederick Douglass was born into slavery in Talbot County, Maryland, either in 1817 or 1818. In his very early years, he lived with his grandmother, called Aunt Betsey. When she was no longer able to work the fields, she retired to a separate farm called Holme Hill to care for a large number of the children of working slaves—a typical arrangement in the plantation economy. Douglass spent his early years exploring the natural environment of the Eastern Shore of Maryland and basking in the love of his devoted grandmother.

When Douglass was six or seven, his grandmother was forced to take him to what was called the Great House, a walking trip of some twelve miles. There, like his brother and five sisters, he was put to work for an employee of wealthy plantation owner Edward Lloyd, a man named Aaron Anthony, called Captain Anthony in the *Narrative*. A widower, Anthony shared his house with his daughter, Lucretia, and her husband, Thomas Auld. There Douglass was introduced to the cruelties of slave life so vividly described in his *Narrative*. His mother, whom he rarely saw, died soon thereafter.

Douglass's Young Life in Baltimore

When he was eight or so, Douglass was sent to Baltimore to serve under Thomas Auld's brother, Hugh, and his wife, Sophia, who lived near the shipbuilding area of this thriving port city. Sophia, who at first was kind to young Douglass, introduced him to reading. Baltimore became the place where he discovered the diverse and exhilarating features of city life. However, his old master, Captain Anthony, died, and his property had to be valued so that it could be divided among the heirs. Douglass was returned to Holme Hill

---

[1] For an excellent biography of Frederick Douglass that treats this material in greater detail see Buchard, Peter. *Frederick Douglass: For the Great Family of Man.* New York: Atheneum Books for Young Readers/Simon and Schuster, 2003.

farm as part of the valuation—an outrage movingly described in the *Narrative*.

Fortunately, he was returned to the Auld household in Baltimore, and although Sophia was forbidden by her husband to give him any more reading lessons, he managed to learn, partly through his friendship with a black preacher named Charles Lawson. He became a voracious reader of inspirational literature like the *Columbian Orator*. He also read newspaper accounts of the **Abolitionist Movement**, an alliance of humanitarian groups dedicated to outlawing slavery. Accounts of resistance to British rule by Irish liberator Daniel O'Connell, of Nat Turner's revolt of 1831, and of John Quincy Adams's petition to have slavery outlawed in the District of Columbia inspired Douglass early on to form ideas that would later lead to his celebrated career as the country's leading African-American abolitionist.

Return to the Eastern Shore of Maryland

Before this was to happen, however, at the age of fifteen, Douglass was returned to the Eastern Shore and to his cruel owner, Thomas Auld. It is thought that Thomas probably resented his brother for having such a good laborer, but he resented even more Douglass's efforts to teach other enslaved people to read by setting up a secret school. Laws at that time forbade African Americans, both free and slave, to gather together for such purposes. To punish Douglass, Auld loaned him out to work for one Edward Covey, a known abuser of slaves, reputedly famous for breaking their spirits as one would break an animal. Although Douglass almost came to despair, eventually he was able to assert his manhood and his dignity by besting the cruel Covey in a fight. The experience with Covey strengthened Douglass's resolve to escape.

First Escape Attempt

Covey, no doubt reluctant to do battle again with Douglass, sent him to work on the nearby farm of William Freeland. Although conditions were better there, Douglass formed a firm determination to escape. About a year after coming to the Freeland farm, when he was almost eighteen, Douglass and four friends made their first escape attempt, but—betrayed by an unknown person—they were caught and jailed. Instead of being sold to other slave traders, Douglass was returned to his master, Thomas Auld, who soon sent him back to his brother Hugh in Baltimore.

Working at a shipyard in Baltimore, Douglass encountered unbridled racial bigotry and was beaten nearly to death by fellow workers who were fearful of losing their jobs to enslaved laborers. Typically, the culprits faced no legal consequences, but Auld did find Douglass work at another shipyard. In Baltimore, Douglass again attempted to teach fellow enslaved persons to read, this time with more success.

"The Underground Railroad," by Charles T. Webber, ca.1893. Library of Congress, LPT 4422-A-2. Used by permission.

Marriage and Successful Escape

At a Mental Improvement Society meeting, Douglass made the acquaintance of a free black woman named Anna Murray. He was nineteen, she twenty-four. Anna, who worked as a servant for rich Baltimoreans, plotted and saved money to help Frederick escape. This he did in September of 1838. Disguised as a merchant seaman with false papers, he boarded a train at Baltimore. This was an extremely dangerous move, since many were anxious to reap the reward offered for the return of fugitives. At Wilmington, Delaware, he boarded a steamer heading for Philadelphia, then took another train to New York where he spent the first two nights hiding among crates and barrels. Eventually, he encountered a black sailor named David Ruggles, secretary of an anti-slavery organization, who helped him find food and lodging. He sent for Anna to come north, and they were married in New York on September 15, 1838.

Life in Massachusetts

The couple was advised to go to New Bedford, Massachusetts, where Douglass would find work in the shipyards. From New Bedford, he made the trip to Nantucket, the site of his first famous abolitionist speech. In 1841, he moved to Lynn, Massachusetts, just north of Boston, with Anna and their two children, Rosetta and Lewis. A second son, named after him, would be born the following year. Douglass's *Narrative* ends shortly after his escape, the details of which he did not then reveal for fear of providing too much information to bounty hunters and slave owners. The rest of his very active life is recorded in two later works, *My Bondage and My Freedom* (1855) and *The Life and Times of Frederick Douglass* (1881, revised 1892).

Move to Rochester, New York

Douglass soon became a well-known figure in the abolitionist movement, but during his frequent travels, he did not escape the shameful segregation laws that separated whites from blacks in trains, horse cars, restaurants, and inns. In Rochester, New York, during a lecture tour, Douglass befriended Isaac and Amy Post, Quakers whom he much admired and who influenced him to settle there. Based in this city, he continued his lecture tours, often facing physical threats. In southern Indiana he was once attacked by a mob that threw him off the stage and broke his hand. His eloquence and skill as a speaker were so exceptional that many doubted he had ever been enslaved. In 1845, partly to convince these doubters, he decided to write his memoirs. The work was an immediate success, read by over a million people in America and Britain during the first two years after publication. Along with Harriet Beecher Stowe's *Uncle Tom's Cabin*, published in 1853, Douglass's *Narrative* served to galvanize public opinion against slavery and to stoke the engine that led to the Civil War.

European Tour

The same year that he published the *Narrative*, Douglass made his first trip to Europe, accompanied by a white friend and neighbor, James Buffam. Starting the tour in Dublin, he was thrilled to meet the famous Irish emancipator Daniel O'Connell. His encounter with the Irish poor and with poor workingmen in Britain engaged his sympathy and, like the Reverend Dr. Martin Luther King, Jr., after him, Douglass began to think of human rights as a worldwide struggle. He saw both economic injustice and slavery as offenses to human dignity. Many of Douglass's British supporters wanted him to stay in England and to bring his family there, knowing he was still in danger in the United States as a fugitive slave. Douglass knew that his mission was primarily in America, and he returned to fulfill it. He did consent, however, to the purchase of his freedom by English friends.

The Rochester Years

After returning from his European tour, in 1847, Douglass moved to Rochester, where he started a weekly newspaper of his own called the *North Star*, somewhat over the objections of abolitionist William Lloyd Garrison, who thought it would be too competitive with the *Liberator*. Douglass began to pry himself away from the influence of the New England abolitionists and to make common cause with New York reformers, including women's rights activist Susan B. Anthony. He even attended the first important women's rights convention in

Seneca Falls in 1848 and supported the aims of such famous black women activists as Sojourner Truth and Harriet Tubman.

In Rochester, where his farmhouse served as a "station" on the Underground Railroad, Douglass came to believe that abolition would never be accomplished peacefully. Congress was dominated by southern legislators, and the Supreme Court favored pro-slavery factions, ruling in the Dred Scott decision that black people could never become full citizens. For a time, Douglass was attracted to the militant views of John Brown, who stayed with him for two weeks in Rochester. He refused, however, to join the raid at Harpers Ferry in October of 1859, believing it a strategic folly; nonetheless, he

was named as a co-conspirator, and Governor Wise of Virginia sought his extradition from New York. Douglass spent some time lecturing in Canada and England to avoid danger. He returned only after the favorite of his five children, Annie, died. A brilliant student, Annie had reaped the benefits of Douglass's long and eventually successful attempt to integrate the public schools of Rochester, and her loss was devastating to him.

Douglass in the Civil War Years

When South Carolina troops fired on the federal arsenal at Fort Sumter on April 2, 1861, Douglass rejoiced that the Civil War had begun and hoped that the war would force Abraham Lincoln to take decisive action to end slavery. Unfortunately, from the point of view of antislavery activists, Lincoln declared the war to be about preserving the Union and not about abolishing slavery. Worried about how the nation could absorb four million slaves as free people and about how few military battles were being won by his then chief commander, General McClellan, Lincoln postponed dealing with the slavery question for two years. Eventually Lincoln found courage and signed the final draft of the Emancipation Proclamation on January 1, 1863. Douglass rejoiced that the purpose of the Civil War was now joined to the cause of abolition and further rejoiced that black soldiers would be allowed to serve in the Union army.

Too old himself to fight, Douglass soon became a recruitment officer for the famous 54th Massachusetts Infantry Regiment led by Colonel Robert Shaw. Douglass's son, Lewis, was appointed sergeant major of this regiment. Another son, Charles, joined as well but fell ill and missed the departure of the regiment. He then transferred to the 5th Massachusetts Cavalry.

Many, including Lincoln himself, believed that the inclusion of black troops was critical to northern victory. During the war, Douglass met twice with Lincoln and encouraged him to hold firm on his decision to make the abolition of slavery a part of the war's purpose. Douglass supported Lincoln's successful candidacy for a second term and attended the inaugural ceremony. Stopped at the door by a policeman, Douglass asked someone to let Lincoln know of the attempt to bar him from the White House. Lincoln immediately intervened and welcomed him as a friend.

Believing that the Emancipation Proclamation might be discarded as a war document, Lincoln supported a constitutional amendment to outlaw slavery. The Thirteenth Amendment, which outlawed slavery, was passed on December 6, 1865, seven months after

"Seated Black Soldier, Frock Coat, Gloves, Kepi," between 1860 and 1870. Library of Congress, LC-USZ62-132213. Used by permission.

"Drawing of an African-American Union Army Soldier," by Alfred R. Waud, between 1862 and 1865. Library of Congress, LC-USZ62-102267. Used by permission.

Lincoln was assassinated. After Lincoln's death, Mary Lincoln sent Douglass the President's favorite walking stick, a memento that Douglass greatly treasured.

The Post Civil War Years

Still in his forties at the end of the Civil War, Douglass continued to be active in the struggle for voting rights and other causes. He campaigned for Ulysses S. Grant for president and was appointed by Grant to a diplomatic post in the Caribbean nation of Santo Domingo (the modern-day Dominican Republic). He moved to Washington, D.C., eventually settling on a fifteen-acre estate in Anacostia, then an almost rural section of town. His Rochester home was destroyed by a suspicious fire. Active in the Republican Party, he held several public posts, including that of U.S. Marshall for the District of Columbia and that of minister and consul general to Haiti.

Throughout the final decades of his life, Douglass continued to be a popular lecturer, traveling widely throughout the country. Two years after his wife, Anna, died in 1882, he married Helen Pitts, a well-educated white woman who had been his secretary when he was a recorder of deeds in the District of Columbia. The marriage caused much controversy in both the black and white communities.

Even in his later life, Douglass did not shy away from this or other controversies. His death-bed visit to his old "master," Thomas Auld, for example, was criticized by many. Douglass, however, apparently considered his act of forgiveness toward the elderly Auld an ennobling and important deed, though returning to his birthplace for the first time since he left was difficult for him. Throughout his life, Douglass denounced the hypocrisy that led some people to consider themselves good Christians while simultaneously embracing the institution of slavery. At the same time, Douglass accepted as a true expression of religious belief such acts of essentially undeserved forgiveness as the one he extended to Auld. As Douglass grew older, family loyalty became very important to him. He helped his brother reunite with his wife and children who had been sold further south and eventually established them in a home on the Eastern Shore of

Maryland. Douglass also remained in close touch with his four living children.

The Death of Frederick Douglass

Douglass died of a heart attack on February 20, 1895, at his home, Cedar Hill. Earlier that day he had attended a meeting of the National Council of Women in Washington, D.C., where his friend Susan B. Anthony, the famous suffragette, invited him to the platform. His brief remarks earned a rousing ovation, a fitting final day for the great orator. He was buried next to his first wife and his daughter Annie in Rochester's Mt. Hope Cemetery.

Douglass's influence did not end with his death but is felt still, more than a century later. In her foreword to *Escape from Slavery: the Boyhood of Frederick Douglass in His Own Words,* by Michael McCurdy, Coretta Scott King describes the influence that Douglass had on her husband, Martin Luther King, Jr., and declares the *Narrative* to be among the best first-hand accounts of slavery ever written. She asserts, "there is much to learn from the way he used language as a tool for liberation." ■

"Frederick Douglass," ca.1880. Library of Congress, LC-DIG-cwpbh-05089. Used by permission.

Historical Background:
Slavery and the Slave Trade

What Is Slavery?

*We were all ranked together. . . . Men and women, old and
young, married and single, were ranked with horses, sheep,
and swine. There were horses and men, cattle and women,
pigs and children, all holding the same rank in the scale of being.*

—Frederick Douglass

The above quotation offers some sense of the dehumanizing
effects of slavery, a practice that is older than human
civilization and that continues in some parts of the world to
this day, despite its extreme barbarity. Slavery in the United States
had its own particular characteristics, but all forms of slavery are the
same in that one group of people essentially exercises unrestricted
control over another.

One of the most conspicuous aspects of slavery is its sheer
physical brutality. As Douglass pointed out, even when slave
"masters" began their careers with relatively generous natures,
they themselves became dehumanized—the institution made them
increasingly cruel. Speaking of one of his "mistresses," Mrs. Hughes,
Douglass wrote that under slavery's influence, "the tender heart
became stone, and the lamblike disposition gave way to one of tiger-
like fierceness." Why? Because absolute power corrupts absolutely.

Of course, people do not remain in bondage of their own free
will, and so they have to be forced. The desire of slave owners to
maintain their dominance gave rise to a multitude of dreadful torture
devices and perverse practices. The whip was the most common
tool of the master or overseer; its shrill crack echoed in the ears of
victims and witnesses for years afterward. Whipping left the skin
permanently scarred and sometimes led to death.

Physical punishment was but one of the tortures inflicted upon
the slave. The mere memory of a severe beating (or witnessing the
beating of another) haunted the slave for the rest of his life, dulled

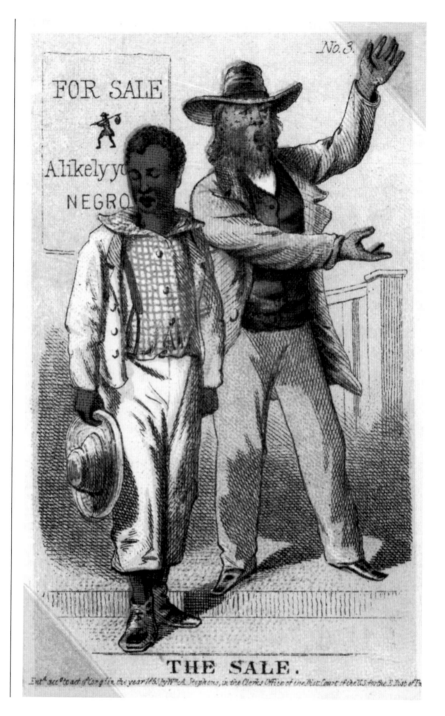

"The Sale," by Henry Louis Stephens, ca.1863. Library of Congress, LC-USZ62-41837. Used by permission.

the emotions and senses, and sometimes left him a mere shell of a human being. Constant hard labor, lack of decent food, and poor living conditions also had emotional, physical, and spiritual impacts. Then there was the threat of separation from family and friends, and the uncertainty as to what hardship the next day might bring. Given the toll that slavery usually took on its victims, it is altogether an astonishing testament to the human spirit that a person like Frederick Douglass could endure its worst and still emerge strong, free, and rational.

Perhaps as you learn more about slavery you will recognize all the privileges and freedoms that we so often take for granted today and be thankful that—no matter how hard you try—you can only begin to imagine the horror of living in hopeless bondage and servitude. And perhaps, as well, you can take courage, yourself, from Douglass's example. Here, truly, was a person unbowed and unafraid.

The Transatlantic Slave Trade

Slavery began in the Western Hemisphere in the early 1500s, as soon as Spanish adventurers began combing the "New World" for its expected caches of gold, silver, and other riches. Early Spanish settlers in the Caribbean and South America exploited native Arawak and Carib Indian populations in order to satisfy their labor needs, and these groups were rapidly annihilated by disease and hardship. By the early 1520s, the Spanish turned to Africa, where Portuguese traders had long ago established ties to existing slave markets along that continent's western coast.

Large-scale transatlantic shipments of African slaves increased sharply in the late sixteenth century with the development of sugar and tobacco plantations in Brazil, Jamaica, and St. Domingue.[2] Later, Cuba was also home to an immense plantation system, as were other parts of the British and French West Indies. Through the mid 1800s, however, Brazil would prove to be by far the single largest importer of

---

[2] **St. Domingue.** Modern Hispaniola, the island shared by Haiti and the Dominican Republic

African slaves, absorbing more than 60 percent of all forced migrants from Africa to the Western Hemisphere.

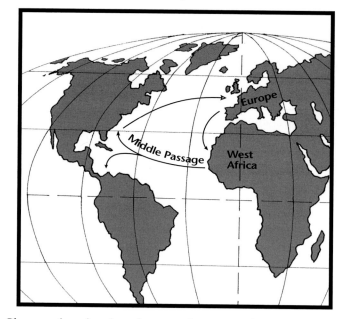

The **Triangle Trade,** depicted in a stylized way in the map to the right, involved ships leaving Europe, traveling to West Africa to take on cargoes of slaves, bringing these slaves to the Americas or the Caribbean, and trading for goods that were then brought back to Europe. The leg of the journey from West Africa to the Americas or the Caribbean was known as the **Middle Passage.**

Slave traders developed a route known as the "Triangle Trade," wherein African slaves were traded in the Americas for raw materials (sugar, molasses, timber, and later, tobacco and cotton), which in turn were shipped to Europe for consumption or processed into manufactured goods. These goods were used to purchase more slaves in Africa, completing the triangle and beginning the process anew.

Many slaves were prisoners of war or victims of raids perpetrated by rival tribes (and sometimes Portuguese traders), who swapped their human commodities for textiles, guns, and other European goods. By the end of the transatlantic slave trade in the mid-nineteenth century, as many as 12 million Africans had been sold into slavery and transported to the Western Hemisphere. Of these, approximately 10 million survived the wretched journey across the Atlantic.

Known commonly as the **Middle Passage,** the trip from Africa to the Americas lasted anywhere from a few weeks to months depending on the point of embarkation and the final destination.

Most slave ships were relatively small merchant vessels that transported one hundred to three hundred slaves, but large ships capable of carrying as many as one thousand slaves were not unusual. Violent mutiny was a constant threat aboard any slave ship, and history records hundreds of such events. Crews took every precaution to prevent uprisings, with swift and severe punishment for rebellious slaves.

Frederick Douglass was born in the United States, so he did not experience the journey from Africa. For firsthand details of the Middle Passage we must turn to other "slave narratives," one of the most famous of which is by Olaudah Equiano, a Nigerian sold into slavery at the age of eleven. In the following passage, Equiano describes being beaten because he refused his food (probably because he was too sick to eat).

Soon, to my grief, two of the white men offered me eatables and on my refusing to eat, one of them held me fast by the hands and laid me across the windlass and tied my feet while the

other flogged me severely. I had never experienced anything of this kind before. If I could have gotten over the nettings, I would have jumped over the side, but I could not. The crew used to watch very closely those of

"The Slave Deck of the Bark *Wildfire,* Brought into Key West on April 30, 1860." Wood engraving illustration from *Harper's Weekly,* June 2, 1860.

us who were not chained down to the decks, lest we should leap into the water.

The conditions aboard a slave vessel—especially one of the very large ones—are virtually unimaginable for modern minds. According to Equiano, "The closeness of the place and the heat of the climate, added to the number of the ship, which was so crowded that each had scarcely room to turn himself, almost suffocated us. . . . The air became unfit for respiration from a variety of loathsome smells, and brought on a sickness among the slaves, of which many died."

Slaves were usually kept in the cargo hold, where chains were available for the unruly, if not for the entire population. Traders

UNITED STATES SLAVE TRADE.
1830.

"The United States Slave Trade, 1830." Engraving. Library of Congress, LC-USZ62-89701. Used by permission.

often modified their cargo holds in order to use every inch of space, allowing perhaps four feet of headroom for the slaves. Thus, slaves led a nightmarish existence in the dark, stuffy cargo holds, awash in human waste, blood, and general misery. As the journey wore on, supplies onboard the ships dwindled, and sickness became rampant, resulting in increased death rates among slaves and crew alike.

Slavery in the English Colonies and United States

English colonies, and later the United States, imported only about 5 percent of all African slaves. Early on, the English relied on indentured servants in colonies like Virginia and Barbados. These were usually young men who agreed to work (essentially as slaves) for several years in return for passage, housing, and food. As riches from the "New World" were transferred overseas, the economies and opportunities in Europe improved, and the pool of willing indentured servants dried up. This development, together with a soaring worldwide demand for sugar and cotton, caused planters in the English colonies to follow the lead of their counterparts in the Caribbean and South America to meet their labor needs.

However, slavery in North America developed along entirely different lines than it did in Brazil and other points in the Spanish empire or in the British or French West Indies. Living conditions in North American colonies were relatively easy compared to those in Brazil, where stifling heat, disease, and truly brutal labor practices meant that slaves died almost as quickly as plantation owners could import them from Africa. Also, the vast majority of slaves transported to Brazil and other southern realms were young males (eighteen to thirty years old), which left little chance for the development of families should the slaves live long enough or have the desire to do so. This is not to say that life for a slave in an English colony in North America was not miserable or perilous, but that the ratio of male to female slaves was nearly equal in places like Virginia, and daily life allowed an opportunity for slaves to raise families (though the children were property of the slave owner). By the 1770s, fully 80 percent of slaves in the nascent United States were American born.

The typical landowner in North America also differed fundamentally from his counterparts in Brazil, Cuba, and St. Domingue. Normally, an English settler did not come to the New World intent on making quick riches and returning to Europe to live out his days as an absentee landlord. Instead, the English colonist made his new home in the Americas and had an interest in making sure that his slaves were in relatively good health. By comparison, landowners further south had little direct contact with their plantations and cared little for the slave population as long as profits remained high.

The aftermath of the American Revolution brought the beginning of the antislavery (or Abolitionist) movement, as well as the seeds of division that would eventually lead to the Civil War. The revolution sparked new ways of thinking among Americans, many of whom were uncomfortable with the notion of human bondage in a nation that proclaimed to the rest of the world that "all men are created equal."

Slavery was abolished or gradually phased out in the northern states during the late eighteenth and early nineteenth centuries. In New York, Delaware, and Pennsylvania, laws were passed whereby slaves would be freed within a certain number of years or once they reached a certain age. Furthermore, significant antislavery measures were enacted by Congress, including the Northwest Ordinance of 1787 that prohibited slavery in northwestern territories and a law in 1808 that finally put an end to the importation of African slaves.

At the same time, slave ownership was considered a sacred property right by second- and third-generation slave owners living in the southern states, where roughly 90 percent of slaves were held. In northern states, slave owners normally owned no more than five slaves, who worked as house servants, drivers, handymen, and the like. In the South, however, slaves were the backbone of the agrarian economy. Slave owners saw themselves as guardians of their slaves, believing not only in the inferiority of the African race, but also in their inherent responsibility as slave owners to see to the needs of their human "property."

Plantation Life in the United States

The average plantation in Georgia, South Carolina, and other southern states held about fifty slaves, though this number could range from just a few to several hundred. Large-scale insurrections were rare, in part because of the tight restrictions placed on slave movement and communication with neighboring plantations.

Although most slave owners did not believe themselves to be overtly abusive, the established system was nonetheless cruel and inhumane. Slave owners employed a variety of methods, but the whip was the most common tool for administering punishment or simply letting the slave know who was in charge. Punishments and practices varied from plantation to plantation; whereas twelve lashes of the whip might be sufficient to one master, another master might see fit to administer a hundred or more for the same offense.

A slave family's "quarters" normally consisted of dirt floors, thin walls, and a leaky roof. Enslaved people worked all day, every day, though in most places they were afforded time off on the Sabbath and on certain holidays. Food was basic, with most slaves receiving a paltry breakfast and an evening meal, which they were often too exhausted to prepare or consume.

A slave could sometimes earn wages or make a little money by plying a trade or performing odd jobs. Occasionally, if the master was willing, a slave could even afford to buy his or her own freedom. Such opportunities were uncommon, however, in the southern states. Perhaps the cruelest aspect of the southern slavery system was the fact that entire families were the sole property of the plantation owner and could be separated and sold at the master's discretion. This practice was especially brutal because the family was a slave's major refuge from the hardships of life. The importation of slaves from Africa decreased, but the demand for slaves continued to

"Relics of Slavery Days, Slave Quarters at the Hermitage Plantation outside of Savannah, Georgia." Photograph, ca.1900. Library of Congress, LC-USZ62-103292. Used by permission.

rise, especially with the establishment of western slave states like Louisiana and Mississippi. Thus, slave owners and traders became more intent on increasing the number of American-born slaves and less likely to allow slaves to purchase their own freedom.

With the enlargement of the American-born slave population came the development of a distinct culture, which included religion, music, and folklore, all of which provided some refuge for slaves. When families were split and separated, these elements of culture remained and were passed down through the generations to become vital, enduring components of American civilization.

The Rise of Abolitionism

By the early nineteenth century, major powers in Europe had abolished slavery, as had most of the northern states in the U.S. The growth of the Abolitionist Movement fueled further insurrections and escape attempts in the South. Thanks to the efforts of staunch white abolitionists and freed or escaped slaves like Harriet Tubman, Frederick Douglass, and Sojourner Truth, the Underground Railroad, a network of safe houses, provided refuge for fugitive slaves as they sought haven in the free states.

But freedom was not guaranteed, even once a fugitive reached a state where slavery itself had been abolished. In the Dred Scott decision of 1857, the Supreme Court of the United States sided with the precedent that a black person

> *had no rights* which the white man was bound to respect; and that the Negro might justly and lawfully be reduced to slavery for his benefit. He was bought and sold and treated as an ordinary article of merchandise and traffic, whenever profit could be made by it.[3]

Dred Scott, despite having been transported in and out of "free" states, would remain the property of another man. Similarly, the Fugitive Slave Act of 1850 and other laws protected the rights of southern slaveholders to reclaim their property and required that

---

[3] **had no rights . . . made by it.** Dred Scott v. Sandford, 60 U.S. 393 (1857)

"Minerva and Edgar Bendy, Formerly Enslaved Persons." Photograph, part of Portraits of African-American Ex-Slaves from the U.S. Works Progress Administration, Federal Writers' Project Slave Narratives Collections. Library of Congress, LC-USZ62-125169. Used by permission.

law enforcement officials in northern states do their part to return fugitive slaves to their "rightful" owners.

Such laws enraged abolitionists, and helped to increase popular support for their movement. Famous Americans involved in the Abolitionist Movement include Harriet Beecher Stowe (author of *Uncle Tom's Cabin*), John Brown, Angelina Grimke, and, of course, Frederick Douglass, whose autobiography remains among the most important works of American literature. William Lloyd Garrison, an outspoken leader of the Abolitionist Movement, is another activist whose words still inspire us today. In his newspaper, *The Liberator*, he wrote, "Enslave the liberty of but one human being and the liberties of the world are put in peril." Garrison spoke for all opponents of slavery who saw the institution as a threat to the cause of liberty around the world.

By themselves, however, the abolitionists were unable to bring an end to slavery. Achieving this would come at a cost of 600,000 lives, the wounding of hundreds of thousands of people, and the destruction of cities and towns throughout the South in the bloodiest conflict ever to occur on American soil: the Civil War.

Politics was the chief obstacle to freedom for the slaves. Even at the height of the Civil War, President Lincoln was reluctant to issue his Emancipation Proclamation for fear of offending "border" states where slavery was allowed but whose armies remained loyal to the United States. Lincoln's Emancipation Proclamation became law on January 1, 1863, but only after the terrible Battle of Gettysburg, the turning point in the war, did the Union Army begin liberating slaves en masse. Still, thousands of African Americans remained enslaved until the end of the war, unaware or unable to take advantage of Lincoln's decree that "all persons held as slaves within any State or designated part of a State, the people whereof shall then be in rebellion against the United States, shall be then, thenceforward, and forever free."

Two years later, in 1865, Congress formally ended slavery in the United States with the ratification of the Thirteenth Amendment to the Constitution. In 1888, Brazil became the last country in the Western Hemisphere to abolish the evil that had begun there nearly four centuries before in the name of gold, sugar, and profit. ■

Chapter 1

I was born in Tuckahoe, near Hillsborough, and about twelve miles from Easton, in Talbot County, Maryland. I have no accurate knowledge of my age, never having seen any authentic record containing it. By far the larger part of the slaves know as little of their ages as horses know of theirs, and it is the wish of most masters within my knowledge to keep their slaves thus ignorant. I do not remember to have ever met a slave who could tell of his birthday. They seldom come nearer to it than planting-time, harvest-time, cherry-time, spring-time, or fall-time. A want of information concerning my own was a source of unhappiness to me even during childhood. The white children could tell their ages. I could not tell why I ought to be deprived of the same privilege. I was not allowed to make any inquiries of my master concerning it. He deemed all such inquiries on the part of a slave improper and **impertinent,** and evidence of a restless spirit. The nearest estimate I can give makes me now between twenty-seven and twenty-eight years of age. I come to this, from hearing my master say, some time during 1835, I was about seventeen years old.

My mother was named Harriet Bailey. She was the daughter of Isaac and Betsey Bailey, both colored, and quite dark. My mother was of a darker complexion than either my grandmother or grandfather. My father was a white man. He was admitted to be such by all I ever heard speak of my parentage.

Why did Douglass not know his exact age?

Why would a slave owner not want slaves to have "restless spirits"?

Vocabulary in Place

impertinent, *adj.* Rude, inappropriate
Harry was kept after school for answering his teacher in an **impertinent** way.

The opinion was also whispered that my master was my father; but of the correctness of this opinion, I know nothing; the means of knowing was withheld from me. My mother and I were separated when I was but an infant—before I knew her as my mother. It is a common custom, in the part of Maryland from which I ran away, to part children from their mothers at a very early age. Frequently, before the child has reached its twelfth month, its mother is taken from it, and hired out on some farm a considerable distance off, and the child is placed under the care of an old woman, too old for field labor. For what this separation is done, I do not know, unless it be to hinder the development of the child's affection toward its mother, and to **blunt** and destroy the natural affection of the mother for the child. This is the **inevitable** result.

I never saw my mother, to know her as such, more than four or five times in my life; and each of these times was very short in duration, and at night. She was hired by a Mr. Stewart, who lived about twelve miles from my home. She made her journeys to see me in the night, travelling the whole distance on foot, after the performance of her day's work. She was a field hand, and a whipping is the penalty of not being in the field at sunrise, unless a slave has special permission from his or her master to the contrary—a permission which they seldom get, and one that gives to him that gives it the proud name of being a kind master. I do not recollect of ever seeing my mother by the light of day. She was with me in the night. She would lie down with me, and get me to sleep, but long before I waked she was gone. Very little communication ever took place between us. Death soon ended what little we could have while she lived, and with it her hardships and suffering. She died when I was about seven years old, on one of my master's farms, near Lee's

How well did Douglass know his mother? Why?

Vocabulary in Place

blunt, *v.* To make less sharp, deaden
  Grace's apology **blunted** my anger.

inevitable, *adj.* Unavoidable, sure to happen
  Because she scored very high on the entrance exams, it was **inevitable** that Yolanda would get into a good college.

Illustration entitled "The Last Time He Saw His Mother" from *Frederick Douglass, My Bondage and My Freedom.* New York: Miller, Orton and Mulligan, ca.1855. Special Collections, University of Virginia. Used by permission.

Mill. I was not allowed to be present during her illness, at her death, or burial. She was gone long before I knew any thing about it. Never having enjoyed, to any considerable extent, her soothing presence, her tender and watchful care, I received the tidings of her death with much the same emotions I should have probably felt at the death of a stranger.

Called thus suddenly away, she left me without the slightest **intimation** of who my father was. The whisper that my master was my father may or may not be true; and, true or false, it is of but little consequence to my purpose whilst the fact remains, in all its glaring **odiousness**, that slaveholders have ordained, and by law established, that the children of slave women shall in all cases follow the condition of their mothers; and this is done too obviously to administer to their own lusts, and make a gratification of their wicked desires profitable as well as pleasurable; for by this cunning arrangement, the slaveholder, in cases not a few, sustains to his slaves the double relation of master and father.

I know of such cases; and it is worthy of remark that such slaves invariably suffer greater hardships, and have more to contend with, than others. They are, in the first place, a constant offence to their mistress. She is ever disposed to find fault with them; they can seldom do any thing to please her; she is never better pleased than when she sees them under the lash, especially when she suspects her husband of showing to his mulatto[1] children favors which he withholds from his black slaves. The master is frequently compelled to sell this class of his slaves, out of deference to the feelings of his white wife; and, cruel as the deed may strike any one to be, for a man to sell his own children to human flesh-mongers, it is often the dictate of humanity for him to do so; for, unless he does this, he must not only whip them himself, but must stand by and see one white son tie up his brother, of but few shades darker complexion than himself, and ply the gory lash to his naked back; and if he lisp one word of disapproval, it is set down to his parental partiality, and only makes

What peculiar "double" relationship did slave owners often have toward enslaved persons?

What was often the attitude of the "mistress" toward mulatto children?

---

[1] **mulatto.** Having mixed black and white ancestry

Vocabulary in Place
intimation, *n.* Indirect communication, hint I was very annoyed by Margery's **intimation** that I was not studying hard enough. **odiousness,** *n.* Hatefulness The dictator is a person of such **odiousness** that his people are sure to rebel.

a bad matter worse, both for himself and the slave whom he would protect and defend.

Every year brings with it multitudes of this class of slaves. It was doubtless in consequence of a knowledge of this fact, that one great statesman of the south predicted the downfall of slavery by the inevitable laws of population. Whether this prophecy is ever fulfilled or not, it is nevertheless plain that a very different-looking class of people are springing up at the south, and are now held in slavery, from those originally brought to this country from Africa; and if their increase do no other good, it will do away the force of the argument, that God cursed Ham,[2] and therefore American slavery is right. If the lineal descendants of Ham are alone to be scripturally enslaved, it is certain that slavery at the south must soon become unscriptural; for thousands are ushered into the world, annually, who, like myself, owe their existence to white fathers, and those fathers most frequently their own masters.

I have had two masters. My first master's name was Anthony. I do not remember his first name. He was generally called Captain Anthony—a title which, I presume, he acquired by sailing a craft on the Chesapeake Bay. He was not considered a rich slaveholder. He owned two or three farms, and about thirty slaves. His farms and slaves were under the care of an overseer.[3] The overseer's name was Plummer. Mr. Plummer was a miserable drunkard, a profane swearer, and a savage monster. He always went armed with a cowskin and a heavy **cudgel.** I have known him to cut and slash the women's heads so horribly, that even master would be enraged at his cruelty, and would threaten to whip him if he did not mind himself. Master,

Why, according to Douglass, was there "a very different-looking class of people" emerging in the South?

---

[2] **Ham.** In the Biblical story, one of Noah's sons, the descendants of whom were cursed to serve their brothers as slaves; in the nineteenth century and earlier, some people used this story to justify the institution of slavery

[3] **overseer.** Person hired to manage the field slaves

Vocabulary in Place
cudgel, *n.* Short, heavy stick with a rounded end
The **cudgel** was a common weapon in medieval warfare.

however, was not a humane slaveholder. It required extraordinary barbarity on the part of an overseer to affect him. He was a cruel man, hardened by a long life of slave holding. He would at times seem to take great pleasure in whipping a slave. I have often been awakened at the dawn of day by the most heart-rending shrieks of an own aunt of mine, whom he used to tie up to a joist, and whip upon her naked back till she was literally covered with blood. No words, no tears, no prayers, from his **gory** victim, seemed to move his iron heart from its bloody purpose. The louder she screamed, the harder he whipped; and where the blood ran fastest, there he whipped longest. He would whip her to make her scream, and whip her to make her hush; and not until overcome by fatigue, would he cease to swing the blood-clotted cowskin. I remember the first time I ever witnessed this horrible exhibition. I was quite a child, but I well remember it. I never shall forget it whilst I remember any thing. It was the first of a long series of such outrages, of which I was doomed to be a witness and a participant. It struck me with awful force. It was the blood-stained gate, the entrance to the hell of slavery, through which I was about to pass. It was a most terrible spectacle. I wish I could commit to paper the feelings with which I beheld it.

This occurrence took place very soon after I went to live with my old master, and under the following circumstances. Aunt Hester went out one night,—where or for what I do not know,—and happened to be absent when my master desired her presence. He had ordered her not to go out evenings, and warned her that she must never let him catch her in company with a young man, who was paying attention to her belonging to Colonel Lloyd. The young man's name was Ned Roberts, generally called Lloyd's Ned. Why master was so careful of her, may be safely left to **conjecture.** She was a woman of noble form, and of graceful proportions, having very few equals, and

Who was Lloyd's Ned? Why might he be called by such a name? What was his connection to Aunt Hester?

Vocabulary in Place
gory, *adj.* Bloody, wounded Medieval warfare involved close-range, hand-to-hand fighting and was, therefore, extremely **gory.** **conjecture,** *n.* Guess or interpretation made by inference Modern science has proved the **conjecture** of the ancient Greek philosopher Democritus that objects in the world are made up of tiny atoms.

fewer superiors, in personal appearance, among the colored or white women of our neighborhood.

Aunt Hester had not only disobeyed his orders in going out, but had been found in company with Lloyd's Ned; which circumstance, I found, from what he said while whipping her, was the chief offence. Had he been a man of pure morals himself, he might have been thought interested in protecting the innocence of my aunt; but those who knew him will not suspect him of any such virtue. Before he commenced whipping Aunt Hester, he took her into the kitchen, and stripped her from neck to waist, leaving her neck, shoulders, and back, entirely naked. He then told her to cross her hands, calling her at the same time a d—— b——. After crossing her hands, he tied them with a strong rope, and led her to a stool under a large hook in the **joist,** put in for the purpose. He made her get upon the stool, and tied her hands to the hook. She now stood fair for his **infernal** purpose. Her arms were stretched up at their full length, so that she stood upon the ends of her toes. He then said to her, "Now, you d—— b——, I'll learn you how to disobey my orders!" and after rolling up his sleeves, he commenced to lay on the heavy cowskin, and soon the warm, red blood (amid heart-rending shrieks from her, and horrid oaths from him) came dripping to the floor. I was so terrified and horror-stricken at the sight, that I hid myself in a closet, and dared not venture out till long after the bloody transaction was over. I expected it would be my turn next. It was all new to me. I had never seen any thing like it before. I had always lived with my grandmother on the outskirts of the plantation, where she was put to raise the children of the younger women. I had therefore been, until now, out of the way of the bloody scenes that often occurred on the plantation. ▪

Profanity appearing in the original text have here been deleted. —The Editors

---

Vocabulary in Place

joist, *n.* A supporting timber in a floor or ceiling
  If you want to hang that plant, first screw a hook into a **joist** in the ceiling.

infernal, *adj.* Suitable to or found in hell, wicked
  The cats in the alleyway made an **infernal** noise throughout the night.

A Closer Look

Recalling (just the facts)

1. Where was Frederick Douglass born, and who were his parents?
2. How many times did Douglass have contact with his mother? Describe the circumstances of their visits.
3. What was the name of Douglass's first master? Was he considered rich?
4. Had Douglass witnessed many whippings prior to that of Aunt Hester?

Interpreting (delving deeper)

1. Was Douglass likely to be treated better because of the race of his father?
2. Why did slave masters separate children from their mothers?
3. Douglass left several clues in the text to suggest that Captain Anthony had personal reasons for his treatment of Aunt Hester. Why might Captain Anthony have been so cruel to her?
4. What was Douglass's emotional response to witnessing the beating of Aunt Hester?

Synthesizing (putting it all together)

How did the slave owners control the enslaved? Provide at least three examples from the text. ■

Extensions

Writing

The Autobiographical Sketch. A **biography** is the story of a person's life, written by someone else. An **autobiography** is the story of a person's life told by that person. Thus the *Narrative of the Life of Frederick Douglass* is an autobiography because Douglass wrote it himself. If you were to write about Douglass's life, then you would be writing a biography.

Try your hand at writing an autobiographical sketch to tell about an interesting event from your life. Your writing should be at least two or three paragraphs long. Follow these steps to create a rough draft:

— Choose an event from which you learned an important lesson.

— Make some notes for your autobiographical sketch. Begin by writing what lesson you learned. Use a complete sentence.

— Make a complete list of events in the order that they happened.

— Think of interesting, concrete, vivid verbs (action words) and nouns (words that name things) that you can use in your piece. Make a list.

— Write the draft of your piece. Tell the story from beginning to end. You may want to include **dialogue**, or conversation between the people in your piece. If so, put people's words in quotation marks, and begin a new paragraph for each speaker.

— End your piece by telling what lesson you learned.

Edit your rough draft. Try adding details to make it more concrete and interesting. Delete or rework details that are repetitious or dull. Proofread your edited draft for errors in grammar, usage, mechanics, and spelling. Refer to the Proofreading Checklist on pages 172–73.

Make a clean, final copy. Proofread it again. Then share your work with your classmates and your teacher. ■

Extensions

History and Geography

Slavery and Slave Revolts in Haiti. In Chapter 1 of his *Narrative*, Douglass mentions that "one great statesman of the south predicted the downfall of slavery by the inevitable laws of population." Douglass was referring to the burgeoning population of mulatto children, whose mothers were enslaved and whose fathers were slave owners. This quotation raises an interesting point, one that troubles many students of history, who often ask why, if the enslaved so greatly outnumbered the enslavers, the enslaved did not simply overpower their oppressors by sheer weight of numbers.

Even on a modest plantation, the ratio of slaves to owners and overseers was at least five to one; however, it was not unusual to find a ratio of twenty to one or higher, especially in places like Brazil, Cuba, and St. Domingue. Guns played a large part in the ability of the slave owners to maintain order, but guns were not the only reason. Douglass addressed this issue in his *Narrative* by describing the many ways in which slave owners asserted control over the enslaved, from the use of whips to the separation of families to prevent the formation of family bonds.

There is one major exception to the general rule that slave owners were able to suppress virtually every slave uprising, and this is the amazing story of Haiti, which was the first black republic in the world, the first nation in the world founded by self-liberated slaves, and the first Caribbean state to achieve independence. Frederick Douglass had a personal connection to Haiti; he served as U.S. ambassador there from 1889 to 1891. He had great admiration and hope for the Haitian people.

Violent, large-scale slave revolts began in Haiti in the late 1700s, as French slave owners gradually began to lose control over the 1.5 million mostly African-born slaves living under the brutal system that existed there. The Haitians claimed full independence from France in 1804 after a bloody revolution.

Extensions

History and Geography (cont.)

The Haitian Revolution was a major embarrassment to Napoleon's France, and it sent shudders down the spines of slave owners all over the world. In fact, no nation in the world formally recognized Haiti's independence until 1826, and even after that relations remained chilly at best with the United States and most European countries. Slave owners in the southern United States feared that a similar slave uprising would occur there, and for this reason, the Haitian story inspired enslaved persons in the United States to keep hope alive that they would also, one day, achieve freedom.

Haiti has one of the most interesting and troubled histories of any nation in the world. There are too many fascinating facts and anecdotes to mention in this brief treatment. However, there is a great wealth of resources about Haiti on the Internet and in libraries.

Join in a class project on Haiti. Choose a partner. Then, with your partner, choose one of the following topics to research. Do your research, and present your findings to the rest of your class.

- *What is Christopher Columbus's connection to Haiti?*
- *Who were the Arawak Indians? What happened to them?*
- *What made Haiti the richest European colony in the Western Hemisphere during the eighteenth century?*
- *Describe the French slave system in Haiti.*
- *What happened during the Haitian Revolution?*
- *Who were these historical figures, and what roles did they play in Haitian history:*
Toussaint L'Ouverture, Jean Jacques Dessalines, Henri Christophe, Alexandre Petion, Jean-Pierre Boyer? (Choose one.)
- *What was the difference between the Republic of Haiti and the Kingdom of Haiti? How did each come about?*
- *What is the Citadel? Who built it and why?*
- *What happened during the U.S. occupation of Haiti from 1916 to 1935?*
- *Who were "Papa Doc" and "Baby Doc"?*
- *Who is Jean Bertrand Aristide?*

Chapter 2

My master's family consisted of two sons, Andrew and Richard; one daughter, Lucretia; and her husband, Captain Thomas Auld. They lived in one house, upon the home plantation of Colonel Edward Lloyd. My master was Colonel Lloyd's clerk and superintendent. He was what might be called the overseer of the overseers. I spent two years of childhood on this plantation in my old master's family. It was here that I witnessed the bloody transaction recorded in the first chapter; and as I received my first impressions of slavery on this plantation, I will give some description of it, and of slavery as it there existed. The plantation is about twelve miles north of Easton, in Talbot County, and is situated on the border of Miles River. The principal products raised upon it were tobacco, corn, and wheat. These were raised in great abundance; so that, with the products of this and the other farms belonging to him, he was able to keep in almost constant employment a large sloop,[1] in carrying them to market at Baltimore. This sloop was named *Sally Lloyd*, in honor of one of the colonel's daughters. My master's son-in-law, Captain Auld, was master of the vessel; she was otherwise manned by the colonel's own slaves. Their names were Peter, Isaac, Rich, and Jake. These were **esteemed** very highly by the other slaves, and looked upon as the privileged ones of the plantation; for it was no small affair, in the eyes of the slaves, to be allowed to see Baltimore.

Why were the enslaved workers aboard the Sally Lloyd *considered privileged?*

---

[1] **sloop.** A sailboat with a single mast

Vocabulary in Place
esteem, v. To value greatly Because of her lovely voice, Mary was an **esteemed** member of her choir.

Colonel Lloyd kept from three to four hundred slaves on his home plantation and owned a large number more on the neighboring farms belonging to him. The names of the farms nearest to the home plantation were Wye Town and New Design. "Wye Town" was under the overseership of a man named Noah Willis. New Design was under the overseership of a Mr. Townsend. The overseers of these, and all the rest of the farms, numbering over twenty, received advice and direction from the managers of the home plantation. This was the great business place. It was the seat of government for the whole twenty farms. All disputes among the overseers were settled here. If a slave was convicted of any high **misdemeanor,** became unmanageable, or **evinced** a determination to run away, he was brought immediately here, severely whipped, put on board the sloop, carried to Baltimore, and sold to Austin Woolfolk, or some other slave-trader, as a warning to the slaves remaining.[2]

What happened to "unmanageable" slaves?

Here, too, the slaves of all the other farms received their monthly allowance of food, and their yearly clothing. The men and women slaves received, as their monthly allowance of food, eight pounds of pork, or its equivalent in fish, and one bushel of corn meal. Their yearly clothing consisted of two coarse linen shirts; one pair of linen trousers, like the shirts; one jacket, one pair of trousers for winter, made of coarse negro cloth; one pair of stockings; and one pair of shoes, the whole of which could not have cost more than seven dollars. The allowance of the slave children was given to their mothers, or the old women having the care of them. The children unable to work in the field had neither shoes, stockings, jackets, nor

Did the children receive an adequate allowance?

---

[2] **sold to . . . slave trader.** When enslaved persons were sold as punishment, they were often sent further south, where conditions were considered worse. This is where the expression "sold down the river" comes from.

Vocabulary in Place

misdemeanor, *n.* A misdeed; a small offense, less serious than a felony
   Since Rodney's crime was a **misdemeanor,** he received only a small fine.

evince, *v.* To show clearly
   Mozart **evinced** musical genius from an early age.

What happened if the children's shirts were damaged in some way?

trousers, given to them; their clothing consisted of two coarse linen shirts per year. When these failed them, they went naked until the next allowance-day. Children from seven to ten years old, of both sexes, almost naked, might be seen at all seasons of the year.

There were no beds given the slaves, unless one coarse blanket be considered such, and none but the men and women had these. This, however, is not considered a very great privation. They find less difficulty from the want of beds, than from the want of time to sleep; for when their day's work in the field is done, the most of them

What did the enslaved people do when they were not working in the fields? Why did they have so little time to sleep?

having their washing, mending, and cooking to do, and having few or none of the ordinary facilities for doing either of these, very many of their sleeping hours are consumed in preparing for the field the coming day; and when this is done, old and young, male and female, married and single, drop down side by side, on one common bed,— the cold, damp floor,—each covering himself or herself with their miserable blankets; and here they sleep till they are summoned to the field by the driver's horn. At the sound of this, all must rise, and be off

Why did the enslaved workers hurry to work in the field as soon as the horn sounded?

to the field. There must be no halting; every one must be at his or her post; and woe betides them who hear not this morning summons to the field; for if they are not awakened by the sense of hearing, they are by the sense of feeling: no age nor sex finds any favor. Mr. Severe, the overseer, used to stand by the door of the quarter, armed with a large hickory stick and heavy cowskin, ready to whip any one who was so unfortunate as not to hear, or, from any other cause, was prevented from being ready to start for the field at the sound of the horn.

Mr. Severe was rightly named: he was a cruel man. I have seen him whip a woman, causing the blood to run half an hour at the time; and this, too, in the midst of her crying children, pleading for their mother's release. He seemed to take pleasure in manifesting his **fiendish barbarity.** Added to his cruelty, he was a profane swearer.

Vocabulary in Place

fiendish, *adj.* Extremely wicked or cruel
   Only the most **fiendish** of criminals would vandalize our school!

barbarity, *n.* Lack of cultivation or familiarity with civilization, savagery
   Ghenghis Khan was known for his **barbarity** as well as his military genius.

It was enough to chill the blood and stiffen the hair of an ordinary man to hear him talk. Scarce a sentence escaped him but that was commenced or concluded by some horrid oath. The field was the place to witness his cruelty and profanity. His presence made it both the field of blood and of blasphemy. From the rising till the going down of the sun, he was cursing, raving, cutting, and slashing among the slaves of the field, in the most frightful manner. His career was short. He died very soon after I went to Colonel Lloyd's; and he died as he lived, uttering, with his dying groans, bitter curses and horrid oaths. His death was regarded by the slaves as the result of a merciful providence.

Mr. Severe's place was filled by a Mr. Hopkins. He was a very different man. He was less cruel, less profane, and made less noise, than Mr. Severe. His course was characterized by no extraordinary demonstrations of cruelty. He whipped, but seemed to take no pleasure in it. He was called by the slaves a good overseer.

The home plantation of Colonel Lloyd wore the appearance of a country village. All the mechanical operations for all the farms were performed here. The shoemaking and mending, the blacksmithing, cartwrighting, coopering,[3] weaving, and grain-grinding, were all performed by the slaves on the home plantation. The whole place wore a business-like aspect very unlike the neighboring farms. The number of houses, too, **conspired** to give it advantage over the neighboring farms. It was called by the slaves the GREAT HOUSE FARM. Few privileges were esteemed higher, by the slaves of the out-farms, than that of being selected to do errands at the Great House Farm. It was associated in their minds with greatness. A representative could not be prouder of his election to a seat in the American Congress, than a slave on one of the out-farms would be of his election to do errands at the Great House Farm. They regarded

How did the Great House Farm differ from the neighboring farms?

---

[3]**cartwrighting, coopering.** A cartwright is someone who makes or repairs carts and wagons. A cooper makes barrels.

Vocabulary in Place
conspire, *v.* To plan secretly
The boys **conspired** to make sure that Louis would not be chosen as captain.

it as evidence of great confidence reposed in them by their overseers; and it was on this account, as well as a constant desire to be out of the field from under the driver's lash, that they esteemed it a high privilege, one worth careful living for. He was called the smartest and most trusty fellow, who had this honor conferred upon him the most frequently. The competitors for this office sought as **diligently**

to please their overseers, as the office-seekers in the political parties seek to please and deceive the people. The same traits of character might be seen in Colonel Lloyd's slaves, as are seen in the slaves of the political parties.

The slaves selected to go to the Great House Farm, for the monthly allowance for themselves and their fellow-slaves, were

---

Vocabulary in Place

diligently, *adv.* Marked by steady effort
Thea studied so **diligently** that she almost always earned high grades.

---

peculiarly enthusiastic. While on their way, they would make the dense old woods, for miles around, reverberate with their wild songs, revealing at once the highest joy and the deepest sadness. They would compose and sing as they went along, consulting neither time nor tune. The thought that came up, came out—if not in the word, in the sound;—and as frequently in the one as in the other.

Gippy Plantation, Berkeley County, SC, ca.1933. *Historic American Buildings Survey,* Library of Congress, HABS, SC, 8-MONCO.V,4. Used by permission.

They would sometimes sing the most pathetic sentiment in the most **rapturous** tone, and the most rapturous sentiment in the most pathetic tone. Into all of their songs they would manage to weave something of the Great House Farm. Especially would they do this, when leaving home. They would then sing most exultingly the following words:

Vocabulary in Place

rapturous, *adj.* Expressing overwhelming emotion
    The audience was thrilled by Tonya's **rapturous** singing.

I am going away to the Great House Farm!
O, yea! O, yea! O!

This they would sing, as a chorus, to words which to many
would seem unmeaning **jargon**, but which, nevertheless, were full
of meaning to themselves. I have sometimes thought that the mere
hearing of those songs would do more to impress some minds with
the horrible character of slavery, than the reading of whole volumes
of philosophy on the subject could do.

I did not, when a slave, understand the deep meaning of those
rude and apparently **incoherent** songs. I was myself within the
circle; so that I neither saw nor heard as those without might see and
hear. They told a tale of woe which was then altogether beyond my
feeble comprehension; they were tones loud, long, and deep; they
breathed the prayer and complaint of souls boiling over with the
bitterest anguish. Every tone was a testimony against slavery, and
a prayer to God for deliverance from chains. The hearing of those
wild notes always depressed my spirit, and filled me with **ineffable**
sadness. I have frequently found myself in tears while hearing them.
The mere recurrence to those songs, even now, afflicts me; and while
I am writing these lines, an expression of feeling has already found
its way down my cheek. To those songs I trace my first glimmering
conception of the dehumanizing character of slavery. I can never
get rid of that conception. Those songs still follow me, to deepen
my hatred of slavery, and quicken my sympathies for my brethren
in bonds. If any one wishes to be impressed with the soul-killing

---

Vocabulary in Place

jargon, *n.* Incoherent talk; also, the specialized language of a particular group
  Woodworking, like any trade, has its **jargon** words, such as *rifling* and *plane.*

rude, *adj.* Lacking sophistication or refinement
  Abraham Lincoln was born in a **rude** log cabin in Kentucky.

incoherent, *adj.* Lacking connection or sense; said often of speech
  The survivors of the crash were at first **incoherent.**

ineffable, *adj.* Incapable of being expressed or described
  Thinking of her youth, Ms. Giles experienced **ineffable** emotions.

effects of slavery, let him go to Colonel Lloyd's plantation, and, on allowance-day, place himself in the deep pine woods, and there let him, in silence, analyze the sounds that shall pass through the chambers of his soul,—and if he is not thus impressed, it will only be because "there is no flesh in his **obdurate** heart."

I have often been utterly astonished, since I came to the north, to find persons who could speak of the singing, among slaves, as evidence of their contentment and happiness. It is impossible to conceive of a greater mistake. Slaves sing most when they are most unhappy. The songs of the slave represent the sorrows of his heart; and he is relieved by them, only as an aching heart is relieved by its tears. At least, such is my experience. I have often sung to drown my sorrow, but seldom to express my happiness. Crying for joy, and singing for joy, were alike uncommon to me while in the jaws of slavery. The singing of a man cast away upon a desolate island might be as appropriately considered as evidence of contentment and happiness, as the singing of a slave; the songs of the one and of the other are prompted by the same emotion. ▪

Why and how were slave songs often misinterpreted by those who had never been enslaved?

Vocabulary in Place

obdurate, *adj.* Hardened in wrongdoing, stubborn

The wicked queen, **obdurate** to the end, showed no mercy to her subjects even as she was dying.

A Closer Look

Recalling (just the facts)

1. What crops were grown on Colonel Lloyd's plantation, and where were they sold?

2. What food and clothing allowance did enslaved adults receive?

3. In what sense was Mr. Severe "rightly named"? Describe his personality and behavior.

4. How did enslaved people feel about going to the Great House on errands?

Interpreting (delving deeper)

1. Was Colonel Lloyd's plantation very productive? How do you know?

2. What constituted a slave's bed? Why, according to Douglass, would the enslaved have had little use for a real bed, if they had one at their disposal?

3. Why did the enslaved consider Mr. Hopkins to be a "good overseer," especially compared to Mr. Severe?

4. Why did the enslaved workers want to go to the Great House? What did they do in order to be chosen for such errands?

Synthesizing (putting it all together)

Describe life on a large, rich plantation. How would it be managed and what kind of commercial and agricultural activities might take place there? Also, what kinds of sights and sounds might you experience there? ■

Extensions

Writing

The Comparison-and-Contrast Paragraph.
Douglass compared the overseers Mr. Severe
and Mr. Hopkins as follows:

> *Mr. Severe's place was filled by a Mr. Hopkins. He was a
> very different man. He was less cruel, less profane, and made
> less noise, than Mr. Severe. His course was characterized by no extraordinary
> demonstrations of cruelty. He whipped, but seemed to take no pleasure in it.
> He was called by the slaves a good overseer.*

This passage clearly shows that both men had the same job, but they
behaved very differently. Mr. Hopkins, for instance, was "less cruel," implying
that Mr. Severe was quite cruel by comparison. What else do you know about
Mr. Severe based on what Douglass says about Mr. Hopkins?

Write a paragraph in which you **compare and contrast** two things.

— Choose two things to compare. For example, you can compare and
   contrast two houses or towns, schools, pets, breakfast cereals, academic
   subjects, or any other items, as long as the two things are related.

— On a separate sheet of paper, make a two-sided table with one column for
   "similarities" and another for "differences." Write two to four notes under
   each category. Had Douglass made a chart, it might have looked like this:

Mr. Hopkins vs. Mr. Severe

Similarities	Differences
• Both were overseers for Colonel Lloyd. • Both whipped the enslaved workers.	• Mr. Hopkins was less cruel and profane. • Mr. Severe took pleasure in whipping the enslaved workers. • The enslaved workers thought Mr. Hopkins was a good overseer.

Extensions

Writing (cont.)

—Once you are satisfied with your chart, write an interesting topic sentence explaining your purpose for writing this paragraph. For instance, instead of simply saying, "I am going to compare two houses," you might write an opening that reads, "My family moved from the house where I was born when I was seven years old. Our second house was much nicer than our first house." In this example, the second sentence is the one that will be the topic sentence of the paragraph.

—Continue writing your paragraph by filling in the information from your "similarities and differences" chart. Vary the structures and lengths of your sentences, and use vivid, personal details whenever possible. Do not write something like, "Our first house was small. Our second house was large." Instead, you might write, "I loved our second house because it had so much more space than our old house."

—End the paragraph by offering your own conclusions about your comparison. Douglass's concluding sentence illustrates the effect that Mr. Hopkins's behavior had on the slaves' attitudes. A paragraph about the two houses might end with "I do not care if I ever see that little old house again."

—Refer to the Revision and Proofreading Checklists on pages 170–73 to finish your work. ■

Extensions

Spirituals and the Code. According to Douglass, the songs of the slaves revealed both "the highest joy and the deepest sadness." Douglass pointed out that singing was one way in which slaves dealt with their burdens and expressed their sorrows. Douglass also pointed out that the slaves' songs were "full of meaning to themselves." Research into the nature of slave songs and spirituals has revealed purposes behind these songs beyond simple expression of emotions. One purpose served by slave songs was the transmission of secret messages by means of what scholars of slavery refer to as **the code**. The code was a secret language in which slaves used people, places, and ideas from the Bible to refer to their own situation. For example, the Bible tells the story of how the Hebrew people were enslaved in Egypt under the rule of a Pharaoh. Eventually, the enslaved Hebrews were released from bondage and led across the Jordan River to freedom. The man who led the Hebrews from captivity was named Moses, and Moses led them to a so-called "promised land" called Canaan. The slaves would sing about these Biblical events but actually be singing about their own lives and circumstances. Examples of songs written in the code include "Swing Low, Sweet Chariot"

> I looked over Jordan and what did I see
> Coming for to carry me home?
> A band of angels coming after me,
> Coming for to carry me home.

and "Go Down, Moses"

> Go down, Moses,
> Way down in Egypt's land.
> Tell ole Pharaoh,
> Let my people go.

Extensions

and "Steal Away"

Steal away,

Steal away.

Steal away to Jesus!

Steal away,

Steal away home,

I ain't got long to stay here!

This code was a kind of **extended metaphor**, or **allegory**, in which one set of things stood for another set of things.

Element from Song	Real-life Equivalent
Jordan River	The Ohio River (which separated the North, and freedom, from the South, and slavery)
Moses	People like Harriet Tubman who helped slaves escape and led them to freedom
Pharoah	The slave owner
Chariot	Horse or other means of conveyance
The drinking gourd	The Big Dipper constellation, which points to the North Star
Canaan, the promised land, home, over yonder	The free North
Steal away, head home	Escape

The most famous coded song is "Follow the Drinking Gourd." Here are the first four verses from that song. On a separate sheet of paper, write down any words, phrases, or lines that might hold some sort of coded message. For example, to what season does the second verse refer?

Extensions

The explanation is written below, but do not peek.
Try to figure out some of the codes for yourself, first.

> Follow the drinking gourd!
> Follow the drinking gourd!
> For the old man is a-waiting for to carry you to freedom
> If you follow the drinking gourd.
>
> When the sun comes back and the first quail calls,
> Follow the drinking gourd.
> For the old man is a-waiting to carry you to freedom
> If you follow the drinking gourd.
>
> The riverbank makes a very good road,
> The dead trees will show you the way,
> Left foot, peg foot traveling on,
> Follow the drinking gourd.
>
> Where the great river meets the little river,
> Follow the drinking gourd,
> The old man is a-waiting for to carry you to freedom
> If you follow the drinking gourd.

This song was taught to slaves by a famous "conductor" on the Underground Railroad named Peg Leg Joe. He was a one-legged ex-sailor who made his living doing odd jobs on various plantations, mainly in Alabama. Peg Leg Joe would teach this song on the plantations that he visited and, sure enough, many slaves would make their escape shortly thereafter.

The "drinking gourd" is actually the Big Dipper constellation, which points to the North Star. "When the sun comes back" refers to springtime. The third verse is about the trail markings that the escapees followed: certain trees along the trail had

Extensions

a painting of a left foot beside a circle (a reference to the marks left by Joe when he walked with his peg leg). By following the rivers, the runaways eventually reached the Ohio River, where other conductors would guide them across and help them on their way.

Do some research on the Internet or in the library to find other spirituals and study these for examples of the code. Look, for example, at the songs "Wade in the Water," "Oh Freedom," "O Canaan," and "Roll, Jordan, Roll." ■

Chapter 3

Colonel Lloyd kept a large and finely cultivated garden, which afforded almost constant employment for four men, besides the chief gardener, Mr. M'Durmond. This garden was probably the greatest attraction of the place. During the summer months, people came from far and near—from Baltimore, Easton, and Annapolis—to see it. It abounded in fruits of almost every description, from the hardy apple of the north to the delicate orange of the south. This garden was not the least source of trouble on the plantation. Its excellent fruit was quite a temptation to the hungry swarms of boys, as well as the older slaves, belonging to the colonel, few of whom had the virtue or the vice to resist it. Scarcely a day passed, during the summer, but that some slave had to take the lash for stealing fruit. The colonel had to resort to all kinds of **stratagems** to keep his slaves out of the garden. The last and most successful one was that of tarring his fence all around; after which, if a slave was caught with any tar upon his person, it was deemed sufficient proof that he had either been into the garden, or had tried to get in. In either case, he was severely whipped by the chief gardener. This plan worked well; the slaves became as fearful of tar as of the lash. They seemed to realize the impossibility of touching TAR without being **defiled**.

Why was the garden a constant source of trouble for the slaves?

Vocabulary in Place

stratagem, *n.* Clever scheme for achieving an objective
  The English teacher employed several **stratagems** to get her students to read more.

defile, *v.* To pollute, make filthy
  The politician attempted to **defile** his opponent's reputation.

Narrative of the Life of Frederick Douglass 27

The colonel also kept a splendid riding equipage.[1] His stable and carriage-house presented the appearance of some of our large city livery establishments.[2]

His horses were of the finest form and noblest blood. His carriage-house contained three splendid coaches, three or four gigs, besides dearborns and barouches of the most fashionable style.

This establishment was under the care of two slaves—old Barney and young Barney—father and son. To attend to this establishment was their sole work. But it was by no means an easy employment; for in nothing was Colonel Lloyd more particular than in the management of his horses. The slightest inattention to these was unpardonable, and was visited upon those, under whose care they were placed, with the severest punishment; no excuse could shield them, if the colonel only suspected any want of attention to his horses—a **supposition** which he frequently indulged, and one which, of course, made the office of old and young Barney a very trying one. They never knew when they were safe from punishment. They were frequently whipped when least deserving, and escaped whipping when most deserving it. Every thing depended upon the looks of the horses, and the state of Colonel Lloyd's own mind when his horses were brought to him for use. If a horse did not move fast enough, or hold his head high enough, it was owing to some fault of his keepers. It was painful to stand near the stable-door, and hear the various complaints against the keepers when a horse was taken out for use. "This horse has not had proper attention. He has not been

Why was it so difficult to work in the stables? Were old Barney and his son punished because they did not do a good job?

---

[1] **equipage.** Equipment, materials, in this case for riding. The term is often used to refer to material and equipment used for military purposes (e.g., *camp equipage* is all the things necessary for an encampment).

[2] **livery establishments.** Places that board and care for horses or that hire out horses and carriages for a fee

Vocabulary in Place
supposition, *n.* An assumption, something supposed
Richard's **supposition** that the substitute teacher would not check the homework proved to be wrong.

sufficiently rubbed and curried, or he has not been properly fed; his food was too wet or too dry; he got it too soon or too late; he was too hot or too cold; he had too much hay, and not enough of grain; or he had too much grain, and not enough of hay; instead of old Barney's attending to the horse, he had very improperly left it to his son." To all these complaints, no matter how unjust, the slave must answer never a word. Colonel Lloyd could not **brook** any contradiction from a slave. When he spoke, a slave must stand, listen, and tremble; and such was literally the case. I have seen Colonel Lloyd make old Barney, a man between fifty and sixty years of age, uncover his bald head, kneel down upon the cold, damp ground, and receive upon his naked and toil-worn shoulders more than thirty lashes at the time. Colonel Lloyd had three sons—Edward, Murray, and Daniel,—and three sons-in-law, Mr. Winder, Mr. Nicholson, and Mr. Lowndes. All of these lived at the Great House Farm, and enjoyed the luxury of whipping the servants when they pleased, from old Barney down to William Wilkes, the coach-driver. I have seen Winder make one of the house-servants stand off from him a suitable distance to be touched with the end of his whip, and at every stroke raise great ridges upon his back.

To describe the wealth of Colonel Lloyd would be almost equal to describing the riches of Job.[3] He kept from ten to fifteen house-servants. He was said to own a thousand slaves, and I think this estimate quite within the truth. Colonel Lloyd owned so many that he did not know them when he saw them; nor did all the slaves of the out-farms know him. It is reported of him, that, while riding

---

[3] **Job** (pronounced jōb). A Biblical character, once rich and powerful, whose faith God tested by subjecting him to many misfortunes

Vocabulary in Place
brook, *v.* Put up with, tolerate
The supervisor made it clear that he would **brook** no laziness on the part of his employees.

along the road one day, he met a colored man, and addressed him in the usual manner of speaking to colored people on the public highways of the south: "Well, boy, whom do you belong to?" "To Colonel Lloyd," replied the slave. "Well, does the colonel treat you well?" "No, sir," was the ready reply. "What, does he work you too hard?" "Yes, sir." "Well, don't he give you enough to eat?" "Yes, sir, he gives me enough, such as it is."

The colonel, after ascertaining where the slave belonged, rode on; the man also went on about his business, not dreaming that he had been conversing with his master. He thought, said, and heard nothing more of the matter, until two or three weeks afterwards. The poor man was then informed by his overseer that, for having found fault with his master, he was now to be sold to a Georgia trader. He was immediately chained and handcuffed; and thus, without a moment's warning, he was snatched away, and forever sundered, from his family and friends, by a hand more unrelenting than death. This is the penalty of telling the truth, of telling the simple truth, in answer to a series of plain questions.

It is partly in consequence of such facts, that slaves, when inquired of as to their condition and the character of their masters, almost universally say they are contented, and that their masters are kind. The slaveholders have been known to send in spies among their slaves, to ascertain their views and feelings in regard to their condition. The frequency of this has had the effect to establish

Why did the enslaved workers always speak favorably of their masters? Do you think they were being sincere?

30

among the slaves the **maxim**, that a still tongue makes a wise head. They **suppress** the truth rather than take the consequences of telling it, and in so doing prove themselves a part of the human family. If they have any thing to say of their masters, it is generally in their masters' favor, especially when speaking to an untried man. I have been frequently asked, when a slave, if I had a kind master, and do not remember ever to have given a negative answer; nor did I, in pursuing this course, consider myself as uttering what was absolutely false; for I always measured the kindness of my master by the standard of kindness set up among slaveholders around us. Moreover, slaves are like other people, and **imbibe** prejudices quite common to others. They think their own better than that of others. Many, under the influence of this prejudice, think their own masters are better than the masters of other slaves; and this, too, in some cases, when the very reverse is true. Indeed, it is not uncommon for slaves even to fall out and quarrel among themselves about the relative goodness of their masters, each contending for the superior goodness of his own over that of the others. At the very same time, they mutually **execrate** their masters when viewed separately. It was so on our plantation. When Colonel Lloyd's slaves met the slaves of Jacob Jepson, they seldom parted without a quarrel about their masters; Colonel Lloyd's slaves contending that he was the richest, and Mr. Jepson's slaves that he was the smartest, and most of a man. Colonel Lloyd's slaves would boast his ability to buy and sell Jacob Jepson.

Why might slaves have bragged about their own "masters" to slaves from other plantations?

Vocabulary in Place

maxim, *n.* A rule of conduct expressed as a saying or proverb
> President Lincoln was fond of this **maxim** from Shakespeare's *Hamlet*: "[u]se every man after his desert, and who shall scape whipping?"

suppress, *v.* To put down, especially by force
> The company was unable to **suppress** the facts about its financial situation.

imbibe, *v.* To drink, to take in
> Children sometimes **imbibe** the prejudices and bad habits of their elders.

execrate, *v.* To denounce, to declare to be hateful
> She will pretend to be your friend and then **execrate** you as soon as you turn your back.

Mr. Jepson's slaves would boast his ability to whip Colonel Lloyd. These quarrels would almost always end in a fight between the parties, and those that whipped were supposed to have gained the point at issue. They seemed to think that the greatness of their masters was transferable to themselves. It was considered as being bad enough to be a slave; but to be a poor man's slave was deemed a disgrace indeed! ▪

A Closer Look

Recalling (just the facts)

1. What was the biggest attraction at Colonel Lloyd's plantation?
2. What did Old Barney and Young Barney do on Colonel Lloyd's plantation?
3. For what purpose did plantation owners use spies?

Interpreting (delving deeper)

1. Why were the enslaved workers at Colonel Lloyd's plantation as "fearful of tar as of the lash"?
2. Why was it so difficult for Young Barney and Old Barney to avoid being beaten? What does this tell you about Colonel Lloyd?
3. Why did the slaves brag about the wealth of their masters and even fight among themselves over which plantation was the richest?

Synthesizing (putting it all together)

Explain why the slaves adopted certain attitudes that were not sincere.

Extensions

Parallelism. Writers can make statements more interesting and memorable by using **parallelism,** or repeated grammatical patterns. The following example makes use of parallel noun phrases: *During the seventeenth century, the French, the Spanish, and the English navies fought one another for control of the Caribbean.* This example makes use of parallel prepositional phrases: *Captain Jones sailed around the African coast, across the Atlantic, and down the Amazon river in a single voyage.* Not using proper parallelism can make sentences sound awkward:

- Maya's stereo is much louder than Juan.
- Ms. Jones rewarded us for our hard work and behaving well.
- There are three things I want to do this summer: eat watermelon, fishing, and learn to water-ski.
- The fire not only burned the forest but also several homes.

Did you notice the mistakes? Read the corrections below to see how these sentences should look with proper parallel construction:

- Maya's stereo is much louder than Juan's.
- Ms. Jones rewarded us for our hard work and good behavior.
- There are three things I want to do this summer: eat watermelon, go fishing, and learn to water-ski.
- The fire burned not only the forest but also several homes.

Rewrite each of the following faulty sentences on a separate piece of paper to correct the faulty parallelism. You might find it useful to copy each sentence and to underline or circle the incorrect section before you try to rewrite it.

Extensions

Writing (cont.)

1. My little brother is messy and can be an annoyance.
2. Lance pulled ahead early, he led most of the way, and finished before anyone else.
3. Kayla's test score was better than Philippe.
4. We learned how to do three things at camp: ride horses, to tie knots, and identifying various trees.
5. Chandra loves drawing, sculpting, and to paint.
6. Listen to the music of the whippoorwills, the crickets, and the sounds that the bullfrogs make.
7. The monks say prayers in the morning, they do it at noon, and in the evening.
8. The rings of Saturn, the boiling hot surface of Venus, and the oceans of Earth that are blue are some of the interesting features of the Solar System.
9. The forests were full of lions and tigers, and bears were also there.
10. The mad scientist made himself invisible, shrank the kids, and was traveling back and forth in time. ▪

Extensions

Maxims. As you learned in this chapter, a **maxim** is a traditional saying that expresses a rule for conduct. Here are some examples of maxims:

Better safe than sorry.

The early bird gets the worm.

Look before you leap.

Practice makes perfect.

Where there's a will there's a way.

Do unto others as you would have them do unto you.

Never leave until tomorrow what you can do today.

Actions speak louder than words.

Let bygones be bygones.

A penny saved is a penny earned.

Read between the lines.

A miss is as good as a mile.

Seize the day.

Don't look a gift horse in the mouth.

A fool and his money are soon parted.

He who hesitates is lost.

Money is the root of all evil.

Necessity is the mother of invention.

There's more than one way to skin a cat.

Writers occasionally have some fun by rewriting traditional sayings in unexpected ways, as follows:

1. Where there's a will there's a won't.

2. A miss is as good as a mister.

Work with a partner. First, come up with a list of five traditional sayings to add to the list given above. Then, choose five traditional sayings from your list and the list above to rewrite in unexpected (and perhaps humorous) ways. ■

Chapter 4

M r. Hopkins remained but a short time in the office of overseer. Why his career was so short, I do not know, but suppose he lacked the necessary severity to suit Colonel Lloyd. Mr. Hopkins was succeeded by Mr. Austin Gore, a man possessing, in an eminent degree, all those traits of character **indispensable** to what is called a first-rate overseer. Mr. Gore had served Colonel Lloyd, in the capacity of overseer, upon one of the out-farms, and had shown himself worthy of the high station of overseer upon the home or Great House Farm.

What characteristics might a "first-rate" overseer have had?

Mr. Gore was proud, ambitious, and persevering. He was artful, cruel, and obdurate. He was just the man for such a place, and it was just the place for such a man. It afforded scope for the full exercise of all his powers, and he seemed to be perfectly at home in it. He was one of those who could torture the slightest look, word, or gesture, on the part of the slave, into **impudence**, and would treat it accordingly. There must be no answering back to him; no explanation was allowed a slave, showing himself to have been wrongfully accused. Mr. Gore acted fully up to the maxim laid down by slaveholders, — "It is better that a dozen slaves should suffer under the lash, than that the overseer should be convicted, in the presence of the slaves, of

---

Vocabulary in Place

indispensable, *adj.* Absolutely necessary; not to be done without or done away with

> Exercise is an **indispensable** part of a healthy lifestyle.

impudence, *n.* Contempt for others or offensively bold behavior, disrespect

> Clyde's **impudence** toward the scout master was enough to get him thrown out of the troop for the rest of the year.

---

having been at fault." No matter how innocent a slave might be— it availed him nothing, when accused by Mr. Gore of any misdemeanor. To be accused was to be convicted, and to be convicted was to be punished; the one always following the other with **immutable** certainty. To escape punishment was to escape accusation; and few slaves had the fortune to do either, under the overseership of Mr. Gore. He was just proud enough to demand the most debasing **homage** of the slave, and quite **servile** enough to crouch, himself, at the feet of the master. He was ambitious enough to be contented with nothing short of the highest rank of overseers, and persevering enough to reach the height of his ambition. He was cruel enough to inflict the severest punishment, artful enough to descend to the lowest trickery, and obdurate enough to be insensible to the voice of a reproving conscience. He was, of all the overseers, the most dreaded by the slaves. His presence was painful; his eye flashed confusion; and seldom was his sharp, shrill voice heard, without producing horror and trembling in their ranks.

Mr. Gore was a **grave** man, and, though a young man, he indulged in no jokes, said no funny words, seldom smiled. His words were in perfect keeping with his looks, and his looks were in perfect keeping with his words. Overseers will sometimes indulge in a witty word, even with the slaves; not so with Mr. Gore. He spoke but to command, and commanded but to be obeyed; he dealt sparingly with his words, and bountifully with his whip, never using the former where the latter would answer as well. When he whipped, he seemed

What does it mean to be "insensible to the voice of a reproving conscience"?

Vocabulary in Place

immutable, *adj.* Unchanging and unchangeable
> In the Declaration of Independence, Thomas Jefferson spoke of natural, **immutable** rights.

homage, *n.* The act of showing honor or respect
> Sir Gawain paid **homage** to King Arthur and followed the code of chivalry.

servile, *adj.* In the manner of a servant, overly submissive
> Enslaved workers were expected to act in a **servile** way toward their overseer.

grave, *adj.* Serious
> At this school it is considered a **grave** offense to copy from someone else's paper.

to do so from a sense of duty, and feared no consequences. He did nothing reluctantly, no matter how disagreeable; always at his post, never inconsistent. He never promised but to fulfil. He was, in a word, a man of the most inflexible firmness and stone-like coolness.

His savage barbarity was equaled only by the consummate coolness with which he committed the grossest and most savage deeds upon the slaves under his charge. Mr. Gore once undertook to whip one of Colonel Lloyd's slaves, by the name of Demby. He had given Demby but few stripes, when, to get rid of the scourging, he ran and plunged himself into a creek, and stood there at the depth of his shoulders, refusing to come out. Mr. Gore told him that he would give him three calls, and that, if he did not come out at the third call, he would shoot him. The first call was given. Demby made no response, but stood his ground. The second and third calls were given with the same result. Mr. Gore then, without consultation or deliberation with any one, not even giving Demby an additional call, raised his musket to his face, taking deadly aim at his standing victim, and in an instant poor Demby was no more. His mangled body sank out of sight, and blood and brains marked the water where he had stood.

A thrill of horror flashed through every soul upon the plantation, excepting Mr. Gore. He alone seemed cool and collected. He was asked by Colonel Lloyd and my old master, why he resorted to this extraordinary expedient. His reply was (as well as I can remember) that Demby had become unmanageable. He was setting a dangerous example to the other slaves,—one which, if suffered to pass without some such demonstration

Detail of an illustration from *Frederick Douglass, My Bondage and My Freedom*. New York: Miller, Orton and Mulligan, ca.1855. Special Collections, University of Virginia. Used by Permission.

on his part, would finally lead to the total **subversion** of all rule and order upon the plantation. He argued that if one slave refused to be corrected, and escaped with his life, the other slaves would soon copy the example; the result of which would be the freedom of the slaves, and the enslavement of the whites. Mr. Gore's defence was satisfactory. He was continued in his station as overseer upon the home plantation. His fame as an overseer went abroad. His horrid crime was not even submitted to judicial investigation. It was committed in the presence of slaves, and they of course could neither institute a suit, nor testify against him; and thus the guilty **perpetrator** of one of the bloodiest and most foul murders goes unwhipped of justice, and uncensured by the community in which he lives. Mr. Gore lived in St. Michael's, Talbot County, Maryland, when I left there; and if he is still alive, he very probably lives there now; and if so, he is now, as he was then, as highly esteemed and as much respected as though his guilty soul had not been stained with his brother's blood.

I speak advisedly when I say this,—that killing a slave, or any colored person, in Talbot County, Maryland, is not treated as a crime, either by the courts or the community. Mr. Thomas Lanman, of St. Michael's, killed two slaves, one of whom he killed with a hatchet, by knocking his brains out. He used to boast of the commission of the awful and bloody deed. I have heard him do so laughingly, saying, among other things, that he was the only benefactor of his country in the company, and that when others would do as much as he had done, we should be relieved of "the d— . . . ."

The wife of Mr. Giles Hicks, living but a short distance from where I used to live, murdered my wife's cousin, a young girl between fifteen and sixteen years of age, mangling her person in the most horrible manner, breaking her nose and breastbone with a stick,

How did Mr. Gore justify his murder of Demby?

What happened to a white person if he or she murdered a black person?

A racist epithet appearing in the original text has here been deleted. —The Editors

---

Vocabulary in Place

subversion, *n.* The act of undermining existing authority
Students should try to avoid **subversion** of discipline in the classroom.

perpetrator, *n.* One responsible for carrying out an action, especially a crime
The policeman arrived just in time to see the **perpetrator** duck into the alley.

so that the poor girl expired in a few hours afterward. She was immediately buried, but had not been in her untimely grave but a few hours before she was taken up and examined by the coroner, who decided that she had come to her death by severe beating. The offence for which this girl was thus murdered was this:—She had been set that night to mind Mrs. Hicks's baby, and during the night she fell asleep, and the baby cried. She, having lost her rest for several nights previous, did not hear the crying. They were both in the room with Mrs. Hicks. Mrs. Hicks, finding the girl slow to move, jumped from her bed, seized an oak stick of wood by the fireplace, and with it broke the girl's nose and breastbone, and thus ended her life. I will not say that this most horrid murder produced no sensation in the community. It did produce sensation, but not enough to bring the murderess to punishment. There was a warrant issued for her arrest, but it was never served. Thus she escaped not only punishment, but even the pain of being arraigned before a court for her horrid crime.

Whilst I am detailing bloody deeds which took place during my stay on Colonel Lloyd's plantation, I will briefly narrate another, which occurred about the same time as the murder of Demby by Mr. Gore. Colonel Lloyd's slaves were in the habit of spending a part of their nights and Sundays in fishing for oysters, and in this way made up the deficiency of their scanty allowance. An old man belonging to Colonel Lloyd, while thus engaged, happened to get beyond the limits of Colonel Lloyd's, and on the premises of Mr. Beal Bondly. At this trespass, Mr. Bondly took offence, and with his musket came down to the shore, and blew its deadly contents into the poor old man.

Mr. Bondly came over to see Colonel Lloyd the next day, whether to pay him for his property, or to justify himself in what he had done, I know not. At any rate, this whole fiendish transaction was soon hushed up. There was very little said about it at all, and nothing done. It was a common saying, even among little white boys, that it was worth a half-cent to kill a ". . . ," and a half-cent to bury one.

A racist epithet appearing in the original text has here been deleted. —The Editors

A Closer Look

Understanding the Selection

Recalling (just the facts)

1. Why did Douglass think that Colonel Lloyd replaced Mr. Hopkins as overseer?

2. Did enslaved laborers ever defend themselves when they were accused of wrongdoing? Why or why not?

3. Why did Mr. Gore murder Demby?

4. Was Mr. Gore fired or punished by the law?

Interpreting (delving deeper)

1. Why was Mr. Gore considered to be a "first-rate" overseer? Use at least two examples from the text to explain your answer.

2. What if a slave was innocent of a crime of which he was accused?

3. How does Demby's murder prove Douglass's assertion that Mr. Gore was always consistent, and that he "never promised but to fulfill"?

4. Was Mr. Gore respected by other overseers and white people in the community? Use evidence from the text to support your answer.

Synthesizing (putting it all together)

Explain the overseers' maxim "It is better that a dozen slaves should suffer under the lash, than that the overseer should be convicted, in the presence of the slaves, of having been at fault." Why do you think this rule was important to men like Mr. Gore? ■

Extensions

Writing

The Character Sketch.

> "His words were in perfect keeping with his looks,
> and his looks were in perfect keeping with his words."

The quotation above is one example of the many ways in which Douglass described the hateful overseer named Mr. Gore. Douglass did not include many physical details about Mr. Gore, but because Douglass was such a fine writer, he was still able to plant an image of this overseer in his readers' minds.

In this exercise you will write a paragraph describing Mr. Gore as you picture him, using your imagination and any clues that you can find within the text.

— First, return to the text and reread the passages that describe Mr. Gore's personality, actions, and appearance. As you read, make notes of important details on a separate sheet of paper.

— Decide what tense (past or present) and point of view (first or third person) you wish to use in your paragraph. You can write a fictional account, in the present or past tense, from the perspective of an enslaved person working under Mr. Gore, or you can simply write from your own point of view describing Mr. Gore.

— Write a topic sentence for your paragraph. [Example: Mr. Gore's appearance matched his personality.]

— Write the rest of the paragraph describing Mr. Gore's facial expressions, physical characteristics (height, weight, hair, etc.), voice, clothing, gait (how he walks), and any other important details. Be as precise as possible, painting a picture with your words as you portray this fearsome, merciless man. Remember, good writing often lies in the smallest details—the scar on the arm, the wrinkle in the forehead, the bulging nose, or the bloodshot eyes.

— Refer to the Revision and Proofreading Checklists on pages 170–73 to finish your work. ■

Extensions

Chiasmus. Do you know this famous line?

Ask not what **your country** can do for **you**—

ask what **you** can do for **your country**.

This line from the inaugural address of President John F. Kennedy is a famous example of **chiasmus** (pronounced ky-az-mus). The word is taken from a Greek verb which means "to mark with two crossing lines, as in the letter *X*" (the letter *chi* in the Greek alphabet). A chiasmus is a clever way to make a point or to emphasize an idea. In a chiasmus, the order of the words in the second of two parallel phrases is reversed. If that definition confuses you, just take another look at the diagram above; notice that the words *you* and *your country* in the second clause have simply been reversed.

Frederick Douglass uses *chiasmi* (the plural of chiasmus) throughout his *Narrative*. Although there is nothing cheerful or fun about his topics, one can imagine that Douglass took some pleasure, as a writer, in concocting chiasmi, and found the chiasmus to be an efficient, effective way to make his point.

Chiasmic phrases were especially useful in describing Mr. Gore, the cruel overseer.

He was just the **man** for such a **place**

and it was just the **place** for such a **man**.

Find the other example of a chiasmus in Chapter 4. Once you have located it, copy it onto a separate sheet of paper, dividing it into two clauses (as in the examples above). Write one clause above the other, and leave enough room to draw your *X*. Underline the words that are reversed and draw a connecting *X* between them.

Extensions

Chiasmi come in several varieties. Chiasmic questions are an age-old favorite of poets and philosophers. The Greek playwright Euripides asked, "Who knows but **life** be that which men call **death**, and **death** what men call **life**?" Punsters and humorists also like to take advantage of chiasmic plays on words. Comedian Groucho Marx once said, "**Money** can't make you **happy**, and **happy** can't make you **money**." Richard Lederer, an American author known for his many books and articles on wordplay, loves to ask questions like, "Why do we **drive** on a **parkway** and **park** on a **driveway**?"

— If you have access to the Internet or a book of famous quotations, find another famous chiasmus, diagram it on a separate sheet of paper, and write a sentence or two explaining why you chose it and what it means to you.

— Try to write your own chiasmus. Use one of the examples above as a model if you need help. ▪

Chapter 5

As to my own treatment while I lived on Colonel Lloyd's plantation, it was very similar to that of the other slave children. I was not old enough to work in the field, and there being little else than field work to do, I had a great deal of leisure time. The most I had to do was to drive up the cows at evening, keep the fowls out of the garden, keep the front yard clean, and run of errands[1] for my old master's daughter, Mrs. Lucretia Auld. The most of my leisure time I spent in helping Master[2] Daniel Lloyd in finding his birds, after he had shot them. My connection with Master Daniel was of some advantage to me. He became quite attached to me, and was a sort of protector of me. He would not allow the older boys to impose upon me, and would divide his cakes with me.

I was seldom whipped by my old master, and suffered little from any thing else than hunger and cold. I suffered much from hunger, but much more from cold. In hottest summer and coldest winter, I was kept almost naked—no shoes, no stockings, no jacket, no trousers, nothing on but a coarse tow linen shirt, reaching only to my knees. I had no bed. I must have perished with cold, but that, the coldest nights, I used to steal a bag which was used for carrying corn to the mill. I would crawl into this bag, and there sleep on the cold, damp, clay floor, with my head in and feet out. My feet have been so cracked with the frost, that the pen with which I am writing might be laid in the gashes.

Did the young Douglass receive everything he needed in order to live comfortably?

---

[1] **run of errands.** Run errands, an archaic usage

[2] **Master.** Not a reference, in this case, to the status of the person as a slave owner. Rather, it is a prefix or title used to refer to a young boy before he comes of age and can be addressed as Mister.

We were not regularly allowanced. Our food was coarse corn meal boiled. This was called MUSH. It was put into a large wooden tray or trough, and set down upon the ground. The children were then called, like so many pigs, and like so many pigs they would come and devour the mush; some with oyster shells, others with pieces of shingle, some with naked hands, and none with spoons. He that ate fastest got most; he that was strongest secured the best place; and few left the trough satisfied.

I was probably between seven and eight years old when I left Colonel Lloyd's plantation. I left it with joy. I shall never forget the **ecstasy** with which I received the intelligence that my old master (Anthony) had determined to let me go to Baltimore, to live with Mr. Hugh Auld, brother to my old master's son-in-law, Captain Thomas Auld. I received this information about three days before my departure. They were three of the happiest days I ever enjoyed. I spent the most part of all these three days in the creek, washing off the plantation scurf, and preparing myself for my departure.

The pride of appearance which this would indicate was not my own. I spent the time in washing, not so much because I wished to, but because Mrs. Lucretia had told me I must get all the dead skin off my feet and knees before I could go to Baltimore; for the people in Baltimore were very cleanly, and would laugh at me if I looked dirty. Besides, she was going to give me a pair of trousers, which I should not put on unless I got all the dirt off me. The thought of owning a pair of trousers was great indeed! It was almost a sufficient motive, not only to make me take off what would be called by pig-drovers the mange, but the skin itself. I went at it in good earnest, working for the first time with the hope of reward.

Why was young Douglass so determined to scrub himself clean?

The ties that ordinarily bind children to their homes were all suspended in my case. I found no **severe** trial in my departure.

Vocabulary in Place

ecstasy, *n.* Intense joy or delight
  Yolanda was in a state of **ecstasy** when she received a pony for her birthday.

severe, *adj.* Causing great distress, harsh
  A football injury caused Thomas to experience **severe** pain.

Narrative of the Life of Frederick Douglass **47**

Did Douglass miss his old home when he left to go to Baltimore?

My home was charmless; it was not home to me; on parting from it, I could not feel that I was leaving any thing which I could have enjoyed by staying. My mother was dead, my grandmother lived far off, so that I seldom saw her. I had two sisters and one brother, that lived in the same house with me; but the early separation of us from our mother had well nigh blotted the fact of our relationship from our memories. I looked for home elsewhere, and was confident of finding none which I should relish less than the one which I was leaving. If, however, I found in my new home hardship, hunger, whipping, and nakedness, I had the **consolation** that I should not have escaped any one of them by staying. Having already had more than a taste of them in the house of my old master, and having endured them there, I very naturally inferred my ability to endure them elsewhere, and especially at Baltimore; for I had something of the feeling about Baltimore that is expressed in the proverb, that

According to Douglass, was Baltimore more like England or Ireland?

"being hanged in England is preferable to dying a natural death in Ireland." I had the strongest desire to see Baltimore. Cousin Tom, though not **fluent** in speech, had inspired me with that desire by his **eloquent** description of the place. I could never point out any thing at the Great House, no matter how beautiful or powerful, but that he had seen something at Baltimore far exceeding, both in beauty and strength, the object which I pointed out to him. Even the Great House itself, with all its pictures, was far inferior to many buildings in Baltimore. So strong was my desire, that I thought a gratification of it would fully compensate for whatever loss of comforts I should sustain by the exchange. I left without a regret, and with the highest hopes of future happiness.

Vocabulary in Place

consolation, *n.* Comfort
> Even though Harriet's art project did not win first place, being judged most original was some **consolation** to her.

fluent, *adj.* Able to express oneself effortlessly
> Chandra is **fluent** in English and Hindi.

eloquent, *adj.* Vividly or movingly expressive
> Martin Luther King, Jr., gave an **eloquent** speech to a crowd of supporters.

We sailed out of Miles River for Baltimore on a Saturday morning. I remember only the day of the week, for at that time I had no knowledge of the days of the month, nor the months of the year. On setting sail, I walked aft,[3] and gave to Colonel Lloyd's plantation what I hoped would be the last look. I then placed myself in the bows[4] of the sloop, and there spent the remainder of the day in looking ahead, interesting myself in what was in the distance rather than in things near by or behind.

In the afternoon of that day, we reached Annapolis, the capital of the State. We stopped but a few moments, so that I had no time to go on shore. It was the first large town that I had ever seen, and though it would look small compared with some of our New England factory villages, I thought it a wonderful place for its size—more imposing even than the Great House Farm!

We arrived at Baltimore early on Sunday morning, landing at Smith's Wharf, not far from Bowley's Wharf. We had on board the sloop a large flock of sheep; and after aiding in driving them to the slaughterhouse of Mr. Curtis on Louden Slater's Hill, I was conducted by Rich, one of the hands belonging on board of the sloop, to my new home in Alliciana Street, near Mr. Gardner's shipyard, on Fells Point.

Mr. and Mrs. Auld were both at home, and met me at the door with their little son Thomas, to take care of whom I had been given. And here I saw what I had never seen before; it was a white face beaming with the most kindly emotions; it was the face of my new mistress, Sophia Auld. I wish I could describe the rapture that flashed through my soul as I beheld it. It was a new and strange sight to me, brightening up my pathway with the light of happiness. Little Thomas was told, there was his Freddy, —and I was told to take care of little Thomas; and thus I entered upon the duties of my new home with the most cheering prospect ahead.

What was so remarkable about Sophia Auld's face?

I look upon my departure from Colonel Lloyd's plantation as one of the most interesting events of my life. It is possible, and even quite probable, that but for the mere circumstance of being removed

---

[3] **aft.** Toward the rear of the vessel

[4] **bow or bows.** Front section of a ship or boat

Detail of a painting entitled "Baltimore from Federal Hill. A View of Baltimore Harbor," by William James Bennett, ca.1831. Library of Congress, LC-USZC2-1871. Used by permission.

from that plantation to Baltimore, I should have today, instead of being here seated by my own table, in the enjoyment of freedom and the happiness of home, writing this Narrative, been confined in the **galling** chains of slavery. Going to live at Baltimore laid the foundation, and opened the gateway, to all my subsequent prosperity. I have ever regarded it as the first plain manifestation of that kind **providence** which has ever since attended me, and marked my life with so many favors. I regarded the selection of myself as being somewhat remarkable. There were a number of slave children that

---

Vocabulary in Place

galling, *adj.* Causing extreme irritation
> The alley cat's **galling** screeches kept me awake all night.

providence, *n.* Care; divine direction and protection
> Some people believed that the explorers survived the blizzard thanks to an act of **providence**, while others simply attributed it to luck.

---

might have been sent from the plantation to Baltimore. There were those younger, those older, and those of the same age. I was chosen from among them all, and was the first, last, and only choice.

I may be deemed superstitious, and even **egotistical**, in regarding this event as a special interposition of divine Providence in my favor. But I should be false to the earliest sentiments of my soul, if I suppressed the opinion. I prefer to be true to myself, even at the hazard of incurring the **ridicule** of others, rather than to be false, and incur my own abhorrence. From my earliest recollection, I date the entertainment of a deep conviction that slavery would not always be able to hold me within its foul embrace; and in the darkest hours of my career in slavery, this living word of faith and spirit of hope departed not from me, but remained like ministering angels to cheer me through the gloom. This good spirit was from God, and to him I offer thanksgiving and praise. ▪

How did Douglass endure the "darkest hours" of slavery?

Vocabulary in Place

egotistical, *adj.* Conceited, self-centered, or boastful

Kendall's friends believed that he was **egotistical** because he bragged so much about his grades.

ridicule, *n.* Words or actions intended to evoke laughter toward another person

The candidate's comments were the subject of **ridicule** by political cartoonists in newspapers across the nation.

A Closer Look

Understanding the Selection

Recalling (just the facts)

1. What were some of Douglass's duties as an enslaved child?

2. What did the enslaved children eat? To what did Douglass compare the manner in which they were fed?

3. About how old was Douglass when he left Colonel Lloyd's plantation to go to Baltimore?

4. What did Douglass do during the voyage on the sloop?

Interpreting (delving deeper)

1. Were the young children expected to work as hard as the adults?

2. What two aspects of life as a slave on Colonel Lloyd's plantation were hardest for young Douglass?

3. Why did Douglass feel that he had no home? Did he miss his siblings when he left for Baltimore? Explain.

4. What was Douglass's new job when he arrived at the Auld household? How did he feel about his new circumstances?

Synthesizing (putting it all together)

How did Douglass's life at the Auld household differ from his life on Colonel Lloyd's plantation? Give at least two examples from the text to support your answer.

Extensions

Writing

The Personal Narrative Essay. A **narrative essay** is a short work of nonfiction that tells a story of some importance or significance. If the story is about an experience in the writer's own life, it is called a **personal narrative essay**, or simply a **personal essay**. Typically, such an essay includes both the story itself and some reflection or commentary on the significance of the story.

A good personal narrative essay contains, most often, all the elements of any good story. A story usually contains a **central conflict**—some struggle that the main character engages in. It usually takes place in a particular **setting**—at a particular time and place. It usually contains some interesting, clearly drawn **characters**, including the main character, generally the author. The conflict described in the story generally comes to some conclusion, or **resolution**. And, finally, the story has some significance, or meaning, to the author (and, one hopes, to the reader). In other words, there is a main idea or **theme** that the story communicates. Often, this main idea is something that the main character learns as a result of the experience described in the story.

Taken by itself, Chapter 5 of the *Narrative of the Life of Frederick Douglass* provides a fine example of the personal narrative essay. In this essay, Douglass tells of the events that enabled him to break free of his life on Colonel Lloyd's plantation. The elements of this story are described in the chart to the right:

Elements in Douglass's Personal Narrative in Chapter 5

Main character, or **protagonist**	Frederick Douglass
Central conflict	struggle to break away from bonds of slavery on Colonel Lloyd's plantation
Minor characters	Mrs. Lucretia, Cousin Tom, Mr. and Mrs. Auld, young Thomas
Settings	Colonel Lloyd's plantation, the sloop to Baltimore, Annapolis, and Baltimore
Resolution	Frederick went to Baltimore to live at the home of Mr. and Mrs. Auld; he was still enslaved, but his situation was greatly improved.
Themes	Sometimes, even when faced with great difficulties, people are able to keep hope alive. There is a providence that works in the lives of people.

Extensions

Try your hand at writing a personal narrative of your own. Begin by choosing some event in your life that was especially meaningful to you—an event that taught you a lesson or that helped you to grow in some way. Think about what you learned from this event. That will be the theme of your story. Next, complete a **story map**, or plan, for your personal narrative. To do so, simply make a list in a notebook of the following elements of your story:

The main character	you
The central conflict	the struggle that you experienced in the course of your story
The events in the story	everything that happened, in order of occurrence
The setting of the story	the time and place in which it occurred, including details that you can use to make the setting vivid and concrete for your reader
The resolution of the story	what happened to bring the central conflict to an end
The theme	what you learned from experience

Use your notes to write a rough draft of your essay. The rough draft should be at least three or four paragraphs long. Tell the story; then tell what significance the story has—what you learned from it. A narrative essay does not have to have an introductory paragraph. You can simply begin with the first part of your story. However, keep your reader in mind. You may want to begin by letting your reader know a bit about what lies ahead. For example, you might start your essay like this:

When I was five years old and living on my grandfather's farm in Southern Kentucky, something happened that would change my life and the lives of my brothers and sisters forever.

Extensions

After you have written a rough draft of your personal narrative, revise it carefully. Add details to make the events come alive in your reader's mind. These can be details that describe the time and place vividly. They can be details that describe the actions, appearance, and personalities of the people involved in the story.

Use the Revision Checklist on pages 170-71 as you revise your piece. Make sure that it ends by discussing the overall significance of the story.

Proofread your revised draft using the Proofreading Checklist on pages 172-73. Then, make a clean, final copy of your paper and check it once again before sharing it with your teacher and classmates.

Extensions

Figurative Language: Metaphors and Similes. In the final paragraph of Chapter 5, Frederick Douglass wrote, "From my earliest recollection, I date the entertainment of a deep conviction that slavery would not always be able to hold me within its foul embrace." Then he says that faith and the spirit of hope "remained like ministering angels to cheer me through the gloom." In these sentences, Frederick Douglass made use of **figurative language**—language that is not literally true but that is used to express an idea in a colorful and memorable way.

The first sentence uses a type of figurative language known as a metaphor. When using the technique of **metaphor**, a writer or speaker tells about one thing (his or her subject) as though it were something else. In this case, Douglass spoke of slavery as though it were something foul, or disgusting, that embraced him, or held him tightly in its arms.

Metaphor: Speaking of one thing as though it were something else

Actual subject	Subject spoken of
Slavery	A foul embrace

Metaphors and similes are very much alike. In both cases, one thing is compared to something very different. In the case of a metaphor, the comparison is implied. In the case of a **simile**, the comparison is directly made using *like* or *as*.

Here's a simple, step-by-step procedure for writing a metaphor or simile:

1. Think of a subject—something that you want to write about.
2. Think of some characteristic of the subject that you want to emphasize.
3. Think of something very different from your subject that has that characteristic.
4. Write a sentence in which you describe your subject as being that other thing.
5. Write another sentence in which you compare your subject and the other thing using *like* or *as*. (Example: Faith and Hope are like ministering angels.)

Try your hand at this. Use the procedure outlined above to write three metaphors and three similes. ∎

Chapter 6

My new mistress proved to be all she appeared when I first met her at the door,—a woman of the kindest heart and finest feelings. She had never had a slave under her control previously to myself, and prior to her marriage she had been dependent upon her own industry for a living. She was by trade a weaver; and by constant application to her business, she had been in a good degree preserved from the blighting and dehumanizing effects of slavery. I was utterly astonished at her goodness. I scarcely knew how to behave towards her. She was entirely unlike any other white woman I had ever seen. I could not approach her as I was accustomed to approach other white ladies. My early instruction was all out of place. The crouching servility, usually so acceptable a quality in a slave, did not answer when manifested toward her. Her favor was not gained by it; she seemed to be disturbed by it. She did not deem it **impudent** or unmannerly for a slave to look her in the face. The meanest slave was put fully at ease in her presence, and none left without feeling better for having seen her. Her face was made of heavenly smiles, and her voice of **tranquil** music.

But, alas! this kind heart had but a short time to remain such. The fatal poison of irresponsible power was already in her hands, and soon commenced its infernal work. That cheerful eye, under the

Why did Douglass say that he "scarcely knew how to behave towards" Mrs. Auld?

Vocabulary in Place

impudent, *adj.* Disrespectful
  The **impudent** student spoke to his teacher in a flippant tone of voice.

tranquil, *adj.* Composed, calm, free from anxiety
  The slow, pleasant music and the soft breeze put everyone in a **tranquil** mood.

---

influence of slavery, soon became red with rage; that voice, made all of sweet **accord**, changed to one of harsh and horrid **discord**; and that angelic face gave place to that of a demon.

Very soon after I went to live with Mr. and Mrs. Auld, she very kindly commenced to teach me the A, B, C. After I had learned this, she assisted me in learning to spell words of three or four letters. Just at this point of my progress, Mr. Auld found out what was going on, and at once forbade Mrs. Auld to instruct me further, telling her, among other things, that it was unlawful, as well as unsafe, to teach a slave to read. To use his own words, further, he said, "If you give a . . . an inch, he will take an ell.[1] A . . . should know nothing but to obey his master—to do as he is told to do. Learning would SPOIL the best . . . in the world. Now," said he, "if you teach that . . . (speaking of myself) how to read, there would be no keeping him. It would forever unfit him to be a slave. He would at once become unmanageable, and of no value to his master. As to himself, it could do him no good, but a great deal of harm. It would make him discontented and unhappy." These words sank deep into my heart, stirred up sentiments within that lay slumbering, and called into existence an entirely new train of thought. It was a new and special revelation, explaining dark and mysterious things, with which my youthful understanding had struggled, but struggled in vain. I now understood what had been to me a most **perplexing** difficulty—to wit, the white man's power to enslave the black man. It was a grand

Several racist epithets in the original text have been here deleted. —*The Editors*

What new "train of thought" was awakened in Douglass by the actions and comments of Mr. Auld?

---

[1] **ell.** An English measure equal to 45 inches

Vocabulary in Place

accord, *n.* Agreement, harmony
The two nations agreed to act in **accord** with international laws.

discord, *n.* Lack of agreement or harmony
Hayden always waited until after the orchestra had finished tuning to enter concert halls because he had no stomach for **discord**.

perplexing, *adj.* Confusing, puzzling
Mrs. Allio found the crossword puzzle **perplexing**.

achievement, and I prized it highly. From that moment, I understood
the pathway from slavery to freedom. It was just what I wanted, and
I got it at a time when I the least expected it. Whilst I was saddened
by the thought of losing the aid of my kind mistress, I was gladdened
by the invaluable instruction which, by the merest accident, I had
gained from my master. Though conscious of the difficulty of learning
without a teacher, I set out with high hope, and a fixed purpose, at

Illustration entitled
"Mrs. Auld Teaching
Him to Read" from
*Frederick Douglass,
My Bondage and My
Freedom.* New York:
Miller, Orton and
Mulligan, ca.1855.
Special Collections,
University of Virginia.
Used by Permission.

whatever cost of trouble, to learn how to read. The very decided manner with which he spoke, and strove to impress his wife with the evil consequences of giving me instruction, served to convince me that he was deeply sensible of the truths he was uttering. It gave me the best assurance that I might rely with the utmost confidence on the results which, he said, would flow from teaching me to read. What he most dreaded, that I most desired. What he most loved, that I most hated. That which to him was a great evil, to be carefully **shunned**, was to me a great good, to be diligently sought; and the argument which he so warmly urged, against my learning to read, only served to inspire me with a desire and determination to learn. In learning to read, I owe almost as much to the bitter opposition of my master, as to the kindly aid of my mistress. I acknowledge the benefit of both.

I had resided but a short time in Baltimore before I observed a marked difference, in the treatment of slaves, from that which I had witnessed in the country. A city slave is almost a freeman, compared with a slave on the plantation. He is much better fed and clothed, and enjoys privileges altogether unknown to the slave on the plantation. There is a **vestige** of decency, a sense of shame, that does much to curb and check those outbreaks of atrocious cruelty so commonly enacted upon the plantation. He is a desperate slaveholder, who will shock the humanity of his non-slaveholding neighbors with the cries of his **lacerated** slave. Few are willing to incur the **odium** attaching to the reputation of being a cruel master;

Why did Mr. Auld not want Douglass to learn how to read? How did this argument further inspire Douglass?

Why did slave owners in the city treat their slaves differently than slave owners in the country?

Vocabulary in Place

shun, *v.* To purposefully avoid or keep away from
   After dark, Sheila wisely **shunned** poorly lighted areas of her neighborhood.

vestige, *n.* A visible trace, evidence, or sign of something that once existed
   After the eruption, not a **vestige** of the village on the mountainside remained.

lacerated, *past part.* Torn, mangled, or wounded
   The triage nurse examined Mark's **lacerated** arm.

odium, *n.* A state of disgrace resulting from hateful conduct
   Anyone who indulges in racism deserves the **odium** he will surely receive.

60

and above all things, they would not be known as not giving a slave enough to eat. Every city slave holder is anxious to have it known of him, that he feeds his slaves well; and it is due to them to say, that most of them do give their slaves enough to eat. There are, however, some painful exceptions to this rule. Directly opposite to us, on Philpot Street, lived Mr. Thomas Hamilton. He owned two slaves. Their names were Henrietta and Mary. Henrietta was about twenty-two years of age, Mary was about fourteen; and of all the mangled and **emaciated** creatures I ever looked upon, these two were the most so. His heart must be harder than stone, that could look upon these unmoved. The head, neck, and shoulders of Mary were literally cut to pieces. I have frequently felt her head, and found it nearly covered with festering sores, caused by the lash of her cruel mistress. I do not know that her master ever whipped her, but I have been an eye-witness to the cruelty of Mrs. Hamilton. I used to be in Mr. Hamilton's house nearly every day. Mrs. Hamilton used to sit in a large chair in the middle of the room, with a heavy cowskin always by her side, and scarce an hour passed during the day but was marked by the blood of one of these slaves. The girls seldom passed her without her saying, "Move faster, you ——!" at the same time giving them a blow with the cowskin over the head or shoulders, often drawing the blood. She would then say, "Take that, you ——!" —continuing, "If you don't move faster, I'll move you!" Added to the cruel lashings to which these slaves were subjected, they were kept nearly half-starved. They seldom knew what it was to eat a full meal. I have seen Mary contending with the pigs for the offal[2] thrown into the street. So much was Mary kicked and cut to pieces, that she was oftener called "PECKED" than by her name. ▪

Was Mrs. Hamilton's abuse of Mary normal for a city slaveholder?

*Profanity in the original text has here been deleted.
—The Editors*

---

2 **offal.** Refuse and waste parts, especially from a butchered animal

Vocabulary in Place
emaciated, *adj.* Bony; very thin, especially from starvation 　　Many of the models in the fashion magazine look **emaciated.**

A Closer Look

Recalling (just the facts)

1. Describe the character of Sophia Auld when Douglass first arrived in Baltimore.

2. What was Mr. Auld's reaction when he learned that his wife was teaching Douglass to read?

3. Did Mrs. Auld continue to teach Douglass how to read, even after her husband found out about it?

4. How were slaves in the city generally treated differently from those in the country? Provide two examples from the text.

Interpreting (delving deeper)

1. How did Douglass account for the change in Mrs. Auld's personality and her attitude toward him?

2. Why did most slave owners prohibit slaves from learning to read?

3. What effect did Mr. Auld have on Douglass's desire to learn how to read?

4. Why did the city dwellers tend to treat their slaves better than plantation owners?

Synthesizing (putting it all together)

Why did Douglass consider learning to read to be the key to freedom, and how did he come to this realization? ■

Extensions

Writing

A Journal Entry: Knowledge and Power. Hundreds of years before Frederick Douglass lived, back in 1597, a great thinker by the name of Sir Francis Bacon wrote that "Knowledge is power." In Chapter 6 of the *Narrative*, Frederick Douglass told about the slave owner Thomas Auld, who was horrified to learn that his wife was teaching the young Douglass how to read. According to Douglass, Auld told his wife that if a slave were to learn "how to read, there would be no keeping him. It would forever unfit him to be a slave. He would at once become unmanageable, and of no value to his master." This news came as a great revelation to Douglass. Douglass wrote,

> It was a new and special revelation, explaining dark and mysterious things, with which my youthful understanding had struggled, but struggled in vain. I now understood what had been to me a most perplexing difficulty— to wit, the white man's power to enslave the black man. . . . From that moment, I understood the pathway from slavery to freedom.

What Mr. Auld said confirms Francis Bacon's comment. Knowledge is, indeed, power, and that is why slave owners tried to withhold knowledge from their slaves.

Knowledge empowers people. This can be true in your own life as well. Think about something that you would like to accomplish in your life. Then, think about what you will have to know in order to do this. Next, think about how you can gain that knowledge. Write a short journal entry in which you describe one of your life goals, what you will have to know in order to accomplish that goal, and how you can gain the necessary knowledge. ▪

Extensions

Alliteration. Frederick Douglass made his name as one of the country's most eloquent spokesman against slavery. His writings and speeches moved audiences not only because he could speak with authority, from personal experience, but also because he used the language very skillfully. His writing is worth examining closely, because he used many techniques to make it memorable. One of the techniques that Douglass used again and again is alliteration—the repetition of consonant sounds at the beginnings of words. For example, in the first sentence of this chapter, Douglass described Mrs. Auld as

a woman of the finest feelings

A. The following phrases are all taken from this chapter. Each contains one or more examples of alliteration. Copy the phrases onto a sheet of paper. Then circle the words that alliterate.

1. That eye became . . . red with rage
2. sentiments . . . that lay slumbering
3. I set out with high hope
4. What he most dreaded, that I most desired
5. That . . . was to me a great good
6. to inspire me with a desire and determination to learn
7. I acknowledge the benefit of both
8. I have frequently felt her head and found it . . . festering.
9. to curb and check the cruelty so commonly enacted upon the plantation
10. His heart must be harder than stone

B. Find two more examples of alliteration in the chapter. Then write five sentences of your own that contain alliteration. ■

Chapter 7

I lived in Master Hugh's family about seven years. During this time, I succeeded in learning to read and write. In accomplishing this, I was compelled to resort to various stratagems. I had no regular teacher. My mistress, who had kindly commenced to instruct me, had, in compliance with the advice and direction of her husband, not only ceased to instruct, but had set her face against my being instructed by any one else. It is due, however, to my mistress to say of her, that she did not adopt this course of treatment immediately. She at first lacked the depravity indispensable to shutting me up in mental darkness. It was at least necessary for her to have some training in the exercise of irresponsible power, to make her equal to the task of treating me as though I were a brute.

My mistress was, as I have said, a kind and tender-hearted woman; and in the simplicity of her soul she commenced, when I first went to live with her, to treat me as she supposed one human being ought to treat another. In entering upon the duties of a slaveholder, she did not seem to perceive that I sustained to her the relation of a mere **chattel**, and that for her to treat me as a human being was not only wrong, but dangerously so. Slavery proved as injurious to her as it did to me. When I went there, she was a pious, warm, and tender-hearted woman. There was no sorrow or suffering for which she had not a tear. She had bread for the hungry, clothes for the naked, and comfort for every mourner that came within her reach.

What did Douglass mean in saying that it took some time for his "mistress" (Mrs. Auld) to learn how to be a slaveholder?

Vocabulary in Place

chattel, *n.* An article of movable personal property, such as a cow or wagon
Douglass despised the treatment of human beings as **chattel**.

Slavery soon proved its ability to **divest** her of these heavenly qualities. Under its influence, the tender heart became stone, and the lamblike disposition gave way to one of tiger-like fierceness. The first step in her downward course was in her ceasing to instruct me. She now commenced to practice her husband's precepts. She finally became even more violent in her opposition than her husband himself. She was not satisfied with simply doing as well as he had commanded; she seemed anxious to do better. Nothing seemed to make her more angry than to see me with a newspaper. She seemed to think that here lay the danger. I have had her rush at me with a face made all up of fury, and snatch from me a newspaper, in a manner that fully revealed her **apprehension**. She was an **apt** woman; and a little experience soon demonstrated, to her satisfaction, that education and slavery were incompatible with each other.

From this time I was most narrowly watched. If I was in a separate room any considerable length of time, I was sure to be suspected of having a book, and was at once called to give an account of myself. All this, however, was too late. The first step had been taken. Mistress, in teaching me the alphabet, had given me the INCH, and no precaution could prevent me from taking the ELL.

The plan which I adopted, and the one by which I was most successful, was that of making friends of all the little white boys whom I met in the street. As many of these as I could, I converted into teachers. With their kindly aid, obtained at different times and in different places, I finally succeeded in learning to read. When I was sent on errands, I always took my book with me, and by going

---

Vocabulary in Place

divest, *v.* To deprive or rid oneself of, as of rights or property
> Though born a prince, Guatama **divested** himself of earthly possessions.

apprehension, *n.* Uneasy anticipation, dread
> One could almost sense the **apprehension** in the air as the students waited for their test results.

apt, *adj.* Quick to learn and understand
> We knew that Jerome was an **apt** student, but nobody expected him to get a perfect score on the SAT.

one part of my errand quickly, I found time to get a lesson before my return. I used also to carry bread with me, enough of which was always in the house, and to which I was always welcome; for I was much better off in this regard than many of the poor white children in our neighborhood. This bread I used to bestow upon the hungry little **urchins**, who, in return, would give me that more valuable bread of knowledge. I am strongly tempted to give the names of two or three of those little boys, as a testimonial of the gratitude and affection I bear them; but **prudence** forbids;—not that it would injure me, but it might embarrass them; for it is almost an unpardonable offence to teach slaves to read in this Christian country. It is enough to say of the dear little fellows, that they lived on Philpot Street, very near Durgin and Bailey's shipyard. I used to talk this matter of slavery over with them. I would sometimes say to them, I wished I could be as free as they would be when they got to be men. "You will be free as soon as you are twenty-one, BUT I AM A SLAVE FOR LIFE![1] Have not I as good a right to be free as you have?" These words used to trouble them; they would express for me the liveliest sympathy, and **console** me with the hope that something would occur by which I might be free.

I was now about twelve years old, and the thought of being A SLAVE FOR LIFE began to bear heavily upon my heart. Just about

---

[1] **You will be free . . . SLAVE FOR LIFE.** At twenty-one, the white children would become adults, with the full rights of adult citizens.

> In what way was Douglass "better off" than many white children?

> Why did Douglass not want to reveal the names of the boys who helped him learn to read?

Vocabulary in Place

urchin, *n.* Mischievous, playful youngster

In the nineteenth century, Horatio Alger wrote novels about poor street **urchins** who rose to become respected members of society.

prudence, *n.* Wisdom, exercise of good judgment

Julia used **prudence** when she decided to study instead of going to a movie.

console, *v.* To comfort, to relieve of sorrow or grief

Do not underestimate the power of a hug when trying to **console** someone.

this time, I got hold of a book entitled "The Columbian Orator."[2] Every opportunity I got, I used to read this book. Among much of other interesting matter, I found in it a dialogue between a master and his slave. The slave was represented as having run away from his master three times. The dialogue represented the conversation which took place between them, when the slave was retaken the third time. In this dialogue, the whole argument in behalf of slavery was brought forward by the master, all of which was disposed of by the slave. The slave was made to say some very smart as well as impressive things in reply to his master—things which had the desired though unexpected effect; for the conversation resulted in the voluntary emancipation of the slave on the part of the master.

In the same book, I met with one of Sheridan's[3] mighty speeches on and in behalf of Catholic emancipation. These were choice documents to me. I read them over and over again with **unabated** interest. They gave tongue to interesting thoughts of my own soul, which had frequently flashed through my mind, and died away for want of utterance. The moral which I gained from the dialogue was the power of truth over the conscience of even a slaveholder. What I got from Sheridan was a bold denunciation of slavery, and a powerful vindication of human rights. The reading of these documents enabled me to utter my thoughts, and to meet the arguments brought forward to sustain slavery; but while they relieved me of one difficulty, they brought on another even more painful than

---

[2] **The Columbian Orator.** A popular book edited by Caleb Bingham, a Massachusetts educator, containing selected essays and speeches along with rules of oratory

[3] **Richard Brinsley Sheridan.** A famous British playwright of the eighteenth century. Born in Ireland, he was an orator and a supporter of Irish independence from Great Britain. He thought that the Irish should be free to vote and hold public office. Douglass saw many similarities between the subjugation of the Irish by the English and the enslavement of people of African descent.

Vocabulary in Place
unabated, *adj.* Continued at full strength or force The monsoon rains continued with **unabated** intensity for several weeks.

the one of which I was relieved. The more I read, the more I was led to **abhor** and detest my enslavers. I could regard them in no other light than a band of successful robbers, who had left their homes, and gone to Africa, and stolen us from our homes, and in a strange land reduced us to slavery. I **loathed** them as being the meanest as well as the most wicked of men. As I read and contemplated the subject, behold! that very discontentment which Master Hugh had predicted would follow my learning to read had already come, to torment and sting my soul to unutterable anguish. As I writhed under it, I would at times feel that learning to read had been a curse rather than a blessing. It had given me a view of my wretched condition, without the remedy. It opened my eyes to the horrible pit, but to no ladder upon which to get out. In moments of agony, I envied my fellow-slaves for their stupidity. I have often wished myself a beast. I preferred the condition of the meanest reptile to my own. Any thing, no matter what, to get rid of thinking! It was this everlasting thinking of my condition that tormented me. There was no getting rid of it. It was pressed upon me by every object within sight or hearing, animate or inanimate. The silver trump of freedom had roused my soul to eternal wakefulness. Freedom now appeared, to disappear no more forever. It was heard in every sound, and seen in every thing. It was ever present to torment me with a sense of my **wretched** condition. I saw nothing without seeing it, I heard nothing without hearing it, and felt nothing without feeling it. It looked from every star, it smiled in every calm, breathed in every wind, and moved in every storm.

How did learning to read bring pain as well as pleasure?

Vocabulary in Place

abhor, *v.* To regard with horror or hatred, to detest
　Max **abhorred** romances but loved detective novels.

loathe, *v.* To dislike greatly
　The mailman **loathed** dogs more than anything else in the world.

wretched, *adj.* Miserable, unhappy, distressed
　Felix was always an angry, **wretched** little cat, but we loved him anyway.

I often found myself regretting my own existence, and wishing myself dead; and but for the hope of being free, I have no doubt but that I should have killed myself, or done something for which I should have been killed. While in this state of mind, I was eager to hear any one speak of slavery. I was a ready listener. Every little while, I could hear something about the abolitionists. It was some time before I found what the word meant. It was always used in such connections as to make it an interesting word to me. If a slave ran away and succeeded in getting clear, or if a slave killed his master, set fire to a barn, or did any thing very wrong in the mind of a slaveholder, it was spoken of as the fruit of ABOLITION. Hearing the word in this connection very often, I set about learning what it meant. The dictionary afforded me little or no help. I found it was "the act of abolishing;" but then I did not know what was to be abolished. Here I was perplexed. I did not dare to ask any one about its meaning, for I was satisfied that it was something they wanted me to know very little about. After a patient waiting, I got one of our city papers, containing an account of the number of petitions from the north, praying for the abolition of slavery in the District of Columbia, and of the slave trade between the States. From this time I understood the words ABOLITION and ABOLITIONIST, and always drew near when that word was spoken, expecting to hear something of importance to myself and fellow-slaves. The light broke in upon me by degrees. I went one day down on the wharf of Mr. Waters; and seeing two Irishmen unloading a scow[4] of stone, I went, unasked, and helped them. When we had finished, one of them came to me and asked me if I were a slave. I told him I was. He asked, "Are ye a slave for life?" I told him that I was. The good Irishman seemed to be deeply affected by the statement. He said to the other that it was a pity so fine a little fellow as myself should be a slave for life. He said it was a shame to hold me. They both advised me to run away to the north; that I should find friends there, and that I should be free. I pretended not to be interested in what they said, and

How did Douglass figure out the meaning of the word abolition? _What does it mean?_

Why did Douglass pretend not to be interested in the Irishmen's suggestion?

---

4 **scow.** A large, flat-bottomed boat with square ends, used for transporting freight

Abigail Goodwin   Thomas Garrett

Daniel Gibbons   Lucretia Mott

Faithful Workers in the Cause

Illustration entitled "Faithful Workers of the Cause" from *The Underground Railroad*, by William Still, published by Porter and Coates of Philadelphia in 1872. These are a few of the many famous names and faces from the Abolitionist Movement. Special Collections, University of Virginia. Used by Permission.

treated them as if I did not understand them; for I feared they might be **treacherous**. White men have been known to encourage slaves to escape, and then, to get the reward, catch them and return them to their masters. I was afraid that these seemingly good men might use me so; but I nevertheless remembered their advice, and from that time I resolved to run away. I looked forward to a time at which it would be safe for me to escape. I was too young to think of doing so immediately; besides, I wished to learn how to write, as I might have occasion to write my own pass. I consoled myself with the hope that I should one day find a good chance. Meanwhile, I would learn to write.

The idea as to how I might learn to write was suggested to me by being in Durgin and Bailey's shipyard, and frequently seeing the ship carpenters, after hewing, and getting a piece of timber ready for use, write on the timber the name of that part of the ship for which it was intended. When a piece of timber was intended for the

Why did Douglass want to learn how to write?

Vocabulary in Place

treacherous, *adj.* Dangerous, not to be relied on, not trustworthy

We took one look at the **treacherous** old bridge and decided to hike the long way through the canyon.

larboard side, it would be marked thus—"L." When a piece was for the starboard side, it would be marked thus—"S." A piece for the larboard side forward, would be marked thus—"L. F." When a piece was for starboard side forward, it would be marked thus—"S. F." For larboard aft, it would be marked thus—"L. A." For starboard aft, it would be marked thus—"S. A."[5] I soon learned the names of these letters, and for what they were intended when placed upon a piece of timber in the shipyard. I immediately commenced copying them, and in a short time was able to make the four letters named. After that, when I met with any boy who I knew could write, I would tell him I could write as well as he. The next word would be, "I don't believe you. Let me see you try it." I would then make the letters which I had been so fortunate as to learn, and ask him to beat that. In this way I got a good many lessons in writing, which it is quite possible I should never have gotten in any other way. During this time, my copy-book was the board fence, brick wall, and pavement; my pen and ink was a lump of chalk. With these, I learned mainly how to write. I then commenced and continued copying the Italics in Webster's Spelling Book,[6] until I could make them all without looking on the book. By this time, my little Master Thomas had gone to school, and learned how to write, and had written over a number of copy-books. These had been brought home, and shown to some of our near neighbors, and then laid aside. My mistress used to go to class meeting at the Wilk Street meetinghouse every Monday afternoon, and leave me to take care of the house. When left thus, I used to spend the time in writing in the spaces left in Master Thomas's copy-book,[7] copying what he had written. I continued to do this until I could write a hand very similar to that of Master Thomas. Thus, after a long, tedious effort for years, I finally succeeded in learning how to write. ◼

Why did it take Douglass so long to learn how to write?

---

[5] **When a piece . . . marked thus—"S.A."** *Larboard* refers to the left side of the boat, and *starboard* to the right. *Forward* and *aft* refer to the front and rear, respectively.

[6] **Webster's Spelling Book.** The *American Spelling Book,* by Noah Webster, an enormously popular nineteenth-century reference book

[7] **copy-book.** A popular way of teaching writing was to copy the stories and speeches written by famous people into a blank notebook.

A Closer Look

Understanding the Selection

Recalling (just the facts)

1. What did Douglass learn to do in the seven years during which he lived with the Aulds?
2. How did Mrs. Auld try to prevent Douglass from learning how to read?
3. What were two of Douglass's favorite selections from *The Columbian Orator*?
4. What is an abolitionist?

Interpreting (delving deeper)

1. Why did Douglass say that slavery did as much to harm the slaveholder as it did to harm the slave?
2. How did Douglass feel about the white boys who helped him learn how to read?
3. What did the enslaved people of the United States and the Catholics of Ireland have in common?
4. How did the word *abolitionism* save Frederick Douglass's life?

Synthesizing (putting it all together)

1. Explain the following statement: "Mistress, in teaching me the alphabet, had given me the INCH, and no precaution could prevent me from taking the ELL." Why was Douglass so intent on learning to read well?
2. Why did Douglass become more discontent with being a "slave for life" the more he read? ■

Extensions

Writing

The How-to Essay. An **expository essay** is one that provides information. A particular kind of expository essay is the **how-to essay,** which explains to the reader how to do something. How-to essays are quite common. People often write such essays to explain how to use technology. For example, a person might write a how-to essay that explains the process of editing a photograph using photo editing software. A person might write a how-to essay about how to change strings on a guitar, how to pitch a tent, how to repair a bicycle tire, or how to study for a vocabulary test.

Try your hand at writing a how-to essay. Choose one of the following topics or one of your own:

How to make the perfect peanut butter sandwich

How to decorate the perfect room for a kid

How to build a snowman

How to build an awesome sandcastle

How to fly a kite

How to assemble a skateboard

How to make free throws

Follow these steps to write your how-to essay:

—If your reader will need any materials to complete the task, make a list of those materials.

—Make a list of everything that a person has to do in order to complete the task. Be specific. List the steps in order of occurrence, and number each step.

—Review your list. Make sure that you have not left out any important steps.

—Divide the list of steps into parts. If, for example, you want to write about how to bake a birthday cake, you might divide your steps into Part 1: Gathering the ingredients; Part 2: Preparing the cake; Part 3: Preparing the icing; Part 4: Decorating and serving the cake.

Extensions

Writing (cont.)

- Revise your list.
- Create a title for your paper. Make sure to capitalize the first letter in each word except for prepositions (such as *to, of,* and *from*) and conjunctions (such as *and, or, nor, for, but, so,* and *yet*).
- Think of the audience for whom you are writing. Then, write an introductory paragraph that will capture the attention of your audience and interest your readers in the topic.
- Write a separate paragraph for each part of the task. Begin each paragraph with a topic sentence that states its main idea. Fill in the paragraph with sentences that describe the steps to take.
- As you write the body paragraphs for your how-to essay, use transitions to connect your ideas. Transitions that are useful in writing how-to essays include *first, second, third, fourth, fifth, before, after, then, next,* and *finally.*
- Once you have completed your rough draft, revise your essay. Read it over carefully to make sure that you have not left out any necessary steps and that you have not included any unnecessary steps. Make sure that your language is clear. Imagine that you are a reader trying to follow your directions. Revise the paper, using the Revision Checklist on pages 170–71.
- Proofread the revised draft for errors in grammar, usage, mechanics, and spelling. Follow the Proofreading Checklist on pages 172–73.
- Make a clean, final copy of the paper. Proofread it once again. Then share it with your teacher and your classmates. ■

Extensions

History and Geography

The Abolitionist Movement. In the 1820s a Protestant evangelical movement swept the northern United States. This movement, which came to be known as the **Second Great Awakening**, created in many intellectuals the desire to see morality prevail in the political and social spheres. Evangelicalism gave rise to a number of political movements, including the **temperance movement,** which sought to outlaw alcoholic beverages, the **women's suffrage movement,** which sought to give women the vote, and the **abolitionist movement,** which sought to free African Americans from slavery. Of these three movements, the last was the first to achieve success in its major goal.

In 1831, delegates from throughout the United States met in Philadelphia, the birthplace of the Constitution, to form the American Anti-Slavery Society, which produced books and pamphlets and lobbied Congress to end slavery once and for all. Reaction to the abolitionist movement was fierce and extreme. There were anti-abolitionist riots in several cities and murders of abolitionist leaders. Nonetheless, the abolitionists pressed on. Among their many accomplishments was the founding of institutions of higher education for black men and women, including Knox College, the Oneida Institute, and the racially integrated Oberlin College.

By the 1850s, tensions over the issue of slavery had reached a boiling point. The country was deeply divided. The **Fugitive Slave Law of 1850** required federal marshalls to arrest escaped slaves or face stiff fines. The **Kansas-Nebraska Act of 1854** repealed the **Missouri Compromise** (which outlawed slavery north of the 40th parallel) and allowed people in the Kansas and Nebraska territories to vote to accept or reject slavery. In 1857, the Supreme Court ruled in the **Dred Scott Decision** that slaves were property and could not sue in court. Abolitionists had worked to organize a series of

Extensions

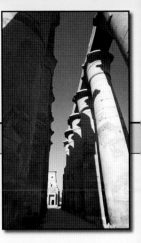

safe houses from the South to the North—the **Underground Railroad**—to help enslaved persons to escape to freedom, but the Dred Scott Decision threatened to undo that great work, for if slaves were property, then slave owners could sue for their return, and no escaped slave was safe. In 1859, abolitionist John Brown led an attack on the federal armory at Harpers Ferry, Virginia, with the hopes of capturing weapons and sparking a slave uprising throughout the South. Brown's small band was defeated, and Brown was hanged. It took a civil war to settle the question of slavery for good. The **Fifteenth Amendment to the Constitution**, ratified on February 3, 1870, stated unequivocally and for all time that "[t]he right of citizens of the United States to vote shall not be denied or abridged by the United States or by any State on account of race, color, or previous condition of servitude."

Many thousands of people participated in the abolitionist movement. Here are some selections from writings by some of the better known abolitionist leaders:

William Ellery Channing, from *Slavery*

I come now to what is to my own mind the great argument against seizing and using a man as property. He cannot be property in the sight of God and justice, because he is a Rational, Moral, Immortal Being; because created in God's image, and therefore in the highest sense his child; because created to unfold godlike faculties, and to govern himself by a Divine Law written on his heart, and republished as God's Word. His whole nature forbids that he should be seized as property. From his very nature it follows, that so to seize him is to offer an insult to his Maker.

Extensions

Salmon P. Chase, from *Warton Jones v. John Vanzandt*, 1846

The law of the Creator, which invests every human being with an inalienable title to freedom, cannot be repealed by any inferior law, which asserts that man is property.

Lydia Maria Child, from *An Appeal in Favor of That Class of Americans Called Africans*

We first debase the nature of man by making him a slave, and then very coolly tell him that he must always remain a slave because he does not know how to use freedom. We first crush people to the earth, and then claim the right of trampling on them forever, because they are prostrate. Truly, human selfishness never invented a rule which worked out so charmingly both ways!

William Lloyd Garrison, from *The Liberator*, January 1, 1831

I am aware that many object to the severity of my language, but is there not cause for severity? I will be harsh as truth, and as uncompromising as justice. On this subject, I do not wish to think, or speak, or write, with moderation. . . . Tell a man whose house is on fire to sound a moderate alarm . . . but urge me not to use moderation. . . . I am in earnest—I will not equivocate—I will not excuse . . . AND I WILL BE HEARD.

Angelina Grimke, from "Appeal to the Christian Women of the Southern States"

It has been justly remarked that "God never made a slave," . . . Slavery always has, and always will produce insurrections wherever it exists, because it is a violation of the natural order of things, and no human power can much longer perpetuate it.

Extensions

Lucretia Mott, exact speech or sermon unknown, ca. 1840

I have no idea of submitting tamely to injustice inflicted either on me or on the slave. I will oppose it with all the moral powers with which I am endowed. I am no advocate of passivity.

Research Assignment: Choose one of the following abolitionists (given here last name first) and research his or her life and work. Prepare a research paper or class presentation on your findings.

Brown, John; Chase, Salmon P.; Child, Lydia Maria; Garrison, William Lloyd; Grimke, Angelina; Grimke, Sarah; Higginson, Thomas W.; Lee, Luther; Mott, Lucretia; Phillips, Wendell; Russwurm, John; Smith, Gerrit; Spooner, Lysander; Stone, Lucy; Sumner, Charles; Tappan, Arthur; Tappan, Lewis; Truth, Sojourner; Tubman, Harriet; Turner, Nat; Vesey, Denmark; Weld, Theodore D.; Whittier, John Greenleaf; Woolman, John; Wright, Jr., Elizur

Chapter 8

Why was Douglass forced to leave Baltimore?

In a very short time after I went to live at Baltimore, my old master's youngest son Richard died; and in about three years and six months after his death, my old master, Captain Anthony, died, leaving only his son, Andrew, and daughter, Lucretia, to share his estate. He died while on a visit to see his daughter at Hillsborough. Cut off thus unexpectedly, he left no will as to the disposal of his property. It was therefore necessary to have a valuation of the property, that it might be equally divided between Mrs. Lucretia and Master Andrew. I was immediately sent for, to be valued with the other property. Here again my feelings rose up in detestation of slavery. I had now a new conception of my degraded condition. Prior to this, I had become, if not insensible to my lot, at least partly so. I left Baltimore with a young heart overborne with sadness, and a soul full of apprehension. I took passage with Captain Rowe, in the schooner[1] Wild Cat, and, after a sail of about twenty-four hours, I found myself near the place of my birth. I had now been absent from it almost, if not quite, five years. I, however, remembered the place very well. I was only about five years old when I left it, to go and live with my old master on Colonel Lloyd's plantation; so that I was now between ten and eleven years old.

We were all ranked together at the valuation. Men and women, old and young, married and single, were ranked with horses, sheep, and swine. There were horses and men, cattle and women, pigs and children, all holding the same rank in the scale of being, and were

---

[1] **schooner.** A sailing vessel with two to seven masts that are fore and aft rigged (i.e., that are found on either side of the mast). These maneuverable cargo ships were very popular in the nineteenth century.

all subjected to the same narrow examination. Silvery-headed age and sprightly youth, maids and matrons, had to undergo the same indelicate inspection. At this moment, I saw more clearly than ever the brutalizing effects of slavery upon both slave and slaveholder.

After the valuation, then came the division. I have no language to express the high excitement and deep anxiety which were felt among us poor slaves during this time. Our fate for life was now to be decided. We had no more voice in that decision than the brutes among whom we were ranked. A single word from the white men was enough—against all our wishes, prayers, and **entreaties**—to sunder[2] forever the dearest friends, dearest kindred, and strongest ties known to human beings. In addition to the pain of separation, there was the horrid dread of falling into the hands of Master Andrew. He was known to us all as being a most cruel wretch,—a common drunkard, who had, by his reckless mismanagement and **profligate dissipation**, already wasted a large portion of his father's property. We all felt that we might as well be sold at once to the Georgia traders, as to pass into his hands; for we knew that that would be our inevitable condition,—a condition held by us all in the utmost horror and dread.

What happened during the "division"?

I suffered more anxiety than most of my fellow-slaves. I had known what it was to be kindly treated; they had known nothing of the kind. They had seen little or nothing of the world. They were in very deed men and women of sorrow, and acquainted with grief.

Why was Douglass more anxious than the other slaves?

---

[2] **sunder.** Tear apart, separate

Vocabulary in Place

entreaty, *n.* Earnest request, plea
  After many **entreaties**, Scott finally persuaded Cyndi to go to the dance.

profligate, *adj.* Recklessly wasteful or extravagant
  Max's **profligate** spending was especially harmful because he bought things for which he had no use.

dissipation, *n.* Wasteful spending or consumption
  The **dissipation** of his bank account caused Max to lose sleep at night

Their backs had been made familiar with the bloody lash, so that they had become callous; mine was yet tender; for while at Baltimore I got few whippings, and few slaves could boast of a kinder master and mistress than myself; and the thought of passing out of their hands into those of Master Andrew—a man who, but a few days before, to give me a sample of his bloody disposition, took my little brother by the throat, threw him on the ground, and with the heel of his boot stamped upon his head till the blood gushed from his nose and ears—was well calculated to make me anxious as to my fate. After he had committed this savage outrage upon my brother, he turned to me, and said that was the way he meant to serve me one of these days,—meaning, I suppose, when I came into his possession.

Thanks to a kind Providence, I fell to the portion of Mrs. Lucretia, and was sent immediately back to Baltimore, to live again in the family of Master Hugh. Their joy at my return equalled their sorrow at my departure. It was a glad day to me. I had escaped a worse than lion's jaws. I was absent from Baltimore, for the purpose of valuation and division, just about one month, and it seemed to have been six.

Very soon after my return to Baltimore, my mistress, Lucretia, died, leaving her husband and one child, Amanda; and in a very short time after her death, Master Andrew died. Now all the property of my old master, slaves included, was in the hands of strangers,— strangers who had had nothing to do with accumulating it. Not a slave was left free. All remained slaves, from the youngest to the oldest. If any one thing in my experience, more than another, served to deepen my conviction of the infernal character of slavery, and to fill me with **unutterable** loathing of slaveholders, it was their base ingratitude to my poor old grandmother. She had served my old master faithfully from youth to old age. She had been the source of all his wealth; she had peopled his plantation with slaves; she had

---

Vocabulary in Place

unutterable, *adj.* Defying description or expression, beyond words

Sir Edmund Hillary felt **unutterable** joy upon reaching the summit of Mt. Everest.

---

a great grandmother in his service. She had rocked him in infancy, attended him in childhood, served him through life, and at his death wiped from his icy brow the cold death-sweat, and closed his eyes forever. She was nevertheless left a slave—a slave for life—a slave in the hands of strangers; and in their hands she saw her children, her grandchildren, and her great-grandchildren, divided, like so many sheep, without being gratified with the small privilege of a single word, as to their or her own destiny. And, to cap the climax of their base ingratitude and fiendish barbarity, my grandmother, who was now very old, having outlived my old master and all his children, having seen the beginning and end of all of them, and her present owners finding she was of but little value, her frame already racked with the pains of old age, and complete helplessness fast stealing over her once active limbs, they took her to the woods, built her a little hut, put up a little mud-chimney, and then made her welcome to the privilege of supporting herself there in perfect loneliness; thus virtually turning her out to die! If my poor old grandmother now lives, she lives to suffer in utter loneliness; she lives to remember and mourn over the loss of children, the loss of grandchildren, and the loss of great-grandchildren. They are, in the language of the slave's poet, Whittier,[3]

Why did Douglass think that his grandmother deserved to be free?

> "Gone, gone, sold and gone
> To the rice swamp dank and lone,
> Where the slave-whip ceaseless swings,
> Where the noisome insect stings,
> Where the fever-demon strews
> Poison with the falling dews,
> Where the sickly sunbeams glare
> Through the hot and misty air: —
> Gone, gone, sold and gone
> To the rice swamp dank and lone,
> From Virginia hills and waters—
> Woe is me, my stolen daughters!"

John Greenleaf Whittier, poet and abolitionist, 1885. Photoprint. Library of Congress, LC-USZ6-227. Used by permission.

---

[3] **Whittier.** This passage is from the poem "The Farewell of a Virginia Slave Mother to her Daughters, Sold into Southern Bondage" (1838). John Greenleaf Whittier was an extremely popular poet and a devoted Quaker abolitionist.

When Douglass was writing his *Narrative*, signs of the trade in human commodities were commonplace along main streets and on farms throughout the southern United States.

Sign carrying the words "Auction and Negro Sales" in Atlanta, Georgia. Photograph by George Bernard, ca.1864. Library of Congress, LC-B811-3608. Used by permission.

"Slave Auction Block, Greenhill Plantation." Campbell County, Virginia. Historic American Buildings Survey. Library of Congress, HABS, VA, 16-LONI.V,1J. Used by permission.

The hearth[4] is desolate. The children, the unconscious children, who once sang and danced in her presence, are gone. She gropes her way, in the darkness of age, for a drink of water. Instead of the voices of her children, she hears by day the moans of the dove, and by night the screams of the hideous owl. All is gloom. The grave is at the door. And now, when weighed down by the pains and aches of old age, when the head inclines to the feet, when the beginning and ending of human existence meet, and helpless infancy and painful old age combine together—at this time, this most needful time, the time for the exercise of that tenderness and affection which children only can exercise towards a declining parent—my poor old grandmother, the devoted mother of twelve children, is left all alone, in yonder little hut, before a few dim embers. She stands—she sits—she staggers— she falls—she groans—she dies—and there are none of her children or grandchildren present, to wipe from her wrinkled brow the cold sweat of death, or to place beneath the sod her fallen remains. Will not a **righteous** God visit for these things?

What did Douglass mean when he said, "The hearth is desolate"?

In about two years after the death of Mrs. Lucretia, Master Thomas married his second wife. Her name was Rowena Hamilton. She was the eldest daughter of Mr. William Hamilton. Master now lived in St. Michael's.[5] Not long after his marriage, a misunderstanding took place between himself and Master Hugh; and as a means of punishing his brother, he took me from him to live with himself at St. Michael's. Here I underwent another most painful separation. It, however, was not so severe as the one I dreaded at the division of property; for, during this interval, a great change

Why was it punishment for Master Hugh when his brother Thomas "took" Douglass to St. Michael's?

---

[4] **hearth.** The floor of a fireplace, usually extending into the room. The word is often used to suggest the entire *home*. See the Extension on page 88.

[5] **St. Michael's.** A small city on the coast of Maryland

Vocabulary in Place
righteous, *n.* Morally upright   Frederick Douglass tried to stir his readers to **righteous** anger.

had taken place in Master Hugh and his once kind and affectionate wife. The influence of brandy upon him, and of slavery upon her, had effected a disastrous change in the characters of both; so that, as far as they were concerned, I thought I had little to lose by the change. But it was not to them that I was attached. It was to those little Baltimore boys that I felt the strongest attachment. I had received many good lessons from them, and was still receiving them, and the thought of leaving them was painful indeed. I was leaving, too, without the hope of ever being allowed to return. Master Thomas had said he would never let me return again. The barrier betwixt himself and brother he considered impassable.

Why did Douglass feel so nervous about being taken away from Baltimore for the second time?

I then had to regret that I did not at least make the attempt to carry out my resolution to run away; for the chances of success are tenfold greater from the city than from the country.

I sailed from Baltimore for St. Michael's in the sloop Amanda, Captain Edward Dodson. On my passage, I paid particular attention to the direction which the steamboats took to go to Philadelphia. I found, instead of going down, on reaching North Point they went up the bay, in a north-easterly direction. I deemed this knowledge of the utmost importance. My determination to run away was again revived. I resolved to wait only so long as the offering of a favorable opportunity. When that came, I was determined to be off.

Why did Douglass care which direction the steamboats were headed?

A Closer Look

Understanding the Selection

Recalling (just the facts)

1. What happened during the "valuation" of Captain Anthony's estate?
2. Why was Douglass afraid that he would be given to Master Andrew?
3. How had Douglass's grandmother contributed to the wealth of those who enslaved her?
4. Why was Douglass removed from Master Hugh in Baltimore and sent to Hugh's brother Thomas in St. Michael's?

Interpreting (delving deeper)

1. What did the valuation process reveal about the way in which enslaved people were treated by slaveholders?
2. Why did Douglass say that he "suffered more anxiety than [his] fellow slaves" during the valuation and division processes?
3. Why did Douglass's grandmother's fate fill him with "unutterable loathing of slaveholders"?
4. How did Douglass feel about being sent away to St. Michael's?

Synthesizing (putting it all together)

Reread the excerpt from the Whittier poem. What is it about? Why did Douglass include it in this chapter? ▨

Extensions

Metonymy. Metonymy is a kind of figurative language in which an object associated with a thing (or a part of a thing) is used to refer to the thing itself.[6] Douglass uses metonymy in this line from Chapter 8: "The hearth is desolate." The hearth is the area in front of a fireplace. However, the term is often used by writers to refer to the entire home. Here are some other examples of metonymy:

> Journalists often use the term *White House* to refer to the entire administration of a president, as in "The White House has yet to take a position on the issue."

> People sometimes use the term *sails* to refer to sailboats, as in "We saw lots of sails coming into the harbor."

Metonymy is a kind of metaphor, in which one thing is used to refer to something else (see the extension on page 56). In the metonymies above, *the hearth* is used to refer to the home, *the White House* is used to refer to a president's administration, and *sails* are used to refer to boats.

Study the sentences given below and on the following page. Each sentence contains one or more examples of metonymy, which are shown in boldface type. Number a sheet of paper from 1 to 20. Next to each number, write what each boldfaced word or phrase stands for. Follow the example given below:

example: All **hands** on deck!

Hands stands for sailors.

1. A little landscape painting in a gallery downtown caught Jamal's **eye.**
2. Chandra was going to do some rock climbing, but at the last minute, she got **cold feet.**

---

[6] **Metonymy . . . itself.** The particular kind of metonymy in which a part is used to refer to a whole is known as **synecdoche.**

Extensions

3. Mr. Colenski was a **factory hand** for many years.

4. Ms. Warneke, the assistant principal, would never **turn a blind eye** to cheating in her school.

5. When Bert saw the new sports car, he said, "Those are some pretty nice **wheels** you have there, Mr. Golem."

6. Ralph said to Cindy, "I only have **eyes** for you."

7. The nurse said to the doctor, "We have **three broken limbs** and **one collarbone fracture** coming in by ambulance."

8. The admiral boasted that there were 124 **masts** in his navy.

9. It's a **long road** from here to Austin, Texas.

10. **Washington** is negotiating a new trade agreement with **Tokyo.**

11. **Hollywood** makes hundreds of movies every year.

12. Our **trumpet** couldn't make it, so we have a sax player filling in.

13. Warren is always sticking his **nose** in where it doesn't belong.

14. **Caesar** conquered Britain.

15. The newspapers suggested that the starlet married for **money.**

16. After we finished the root beers, Maria said, "Can we have three more **glasses,** please?"

17. Why don't we go to Colorado and **hit the slopes?**

18. Yolanda and Paula love **to backpack.**

19. I wanted to find out when the surprise party was, but Paulo was **close-lipped** about it.

20. Elise wanted to take algebra on Tuesday, but **the 9:30** was full. ▪

Extensions

Sensory Images. John Greenleaf Whittier (1807–1892) began his literary career contributing stories and poems to New England newspapers. He is best known for his poem "Snow-Bound," a stunningly beautiful account of the aftermath of a snowstorm in Massachusetts. That poem earned him justifiable wealth and fame. At the time that Douglass was writing his *Narrative*, John Greenleaf Whittier was growing increasingly popular in the abolitionist community.

In his *Narrative*, Douglass quotes the first verse of Whittier's "The Farewell of a Virginia Slave Mother to her Daughters, Sold into Southern Bondage" (1838), one of the poet's most important and dramatic antislavery works. The theme of the poem—the division of families and the cruelty of slavery—is compelling by itself, but it is Whittier's word choice and sensory details that give the poem its heartbreaking power.

The boldfaced words in the following passage are examples of words chosen by the poet specifically to evoke the squalor and physical pain of the slave's life:

> Gone, gone, sold and gone
> To the rice **swamp dank** and **lone,**
> Where the slave-**whip ceaseless** swings,
> Where the **noisome** insect **stings**

The word *swamp* conjures up unpleasant images of an uncomfortable, wet, hot, smelly, and dangerous place. The word *lone* reminds us of the slave's hopeless, isolated existence. We can almost see and hear the cracking whip, followed by the words *noisome* and *stings,* which suggest more irritation and pain. Four lines into this poem, the very thought of slavery should make you sick!

— Reread the rest of the excerpt from this poem in Chapter 8. On a separate sheet of paper, write at least five additional words from the poem that are meant to appeal to the senses. For each word, write a few emotions or feelings that the word brings to mind. For example, for *whip* you could write, Whip: pain, blood, cracking sound, fear ■

Chapter 9

I have now reached a period of my life when I can give dates. I left Baltimore, and went to live with Master Thomas Auld, at St. Michael's, in March, 1832. It was now more than seven years since I lived with him in the family of my old master, on Colonel Lloyd's plantation. We of course were now almost entire strangers to each other. He was to me a new master, and I to him a new slave. I was ignorant of his temper and disposition; he was equally so of mine. A very short time, however, brought us into full acquaintance with each other. I was made acquainted with his wife not less than with himself. They were well matched, being equally mean and cruel. I was now, for the first time during a space of more than seven years, made to feel the painful gnawings of hunger—a something which I had not experienced before since I left Colonel Lloyd's plantation. It went hard enough with me then, when I could look back to no period at which I had enjoyed a sufficiency. It was tenfold harder after living in Master Hugh's family, where I had always had enough to eat, and of that which was good. I have said Master Thomas was a mean man. He was so. Not to give a slave enough to eat, is regarded as the most aggravated development of meanness even among slaveholders. The rule is, no matter how coarse the food, only let there be enough of it. This is the theory; and in the part of Maryland from which I came, it is the general practice,—though there are many exceptions. Master Thomas gave us enough of neither coarse nor fine food. There were four slaves of us in the kitchen—my sister Eliza, my aunt Priscilla, Henny, and myself; and we were allowed less than a half of a bushel of corn-meal per week, and very little else, either in the shape of meat or vegetables. It was not enough for us to subsist upon. We were therefore reduced to the wretched necessity of living at the expense of our neighbors. This we did by begging

How did Douglass and the other enslaved people make up for the lack of food provided by Captain Auld?

and stealing, whichever came handy in the time of need, the one being considered as legitimate as the other. A great many times have we poor creatures been nearly perishing with hunger, when food in abundance lay mouldering in the safe and smoke-house,[1] and our pious mistress was aware of the fact; and yet that mistress and her husband would kneel every morning, and pray that God would bless them in basket and store!

Bad as all slaveholders are, we seldom meet one **destitute** of every element of character commanding respect. My master was one of this rare sort. I do not know of one single noble act ever performed by him. The leading trait in his character was meanness; and if there were any other element in his nature, it was made subject to this. He was mean; and, like most other mean men, he lacked the ability to conceal his meanness. Captain Auld was not born a slaveholder. He had been a poor man, master only of a Bay craft.[2] He came into possession of all his slaves by marriage; and of all men, adopted slaveholders are the worst. He was cruel, but cowardly. He commanded without firmness. In the enforcement of his rules, he was at times **rigid**, and at times **lax**. At times, he spoke to his slaves with the firmness of Napoleon[3] and the fury of a demon; at other times, he might well be mistaken for an inquirer who had lost his way.

How did the fact that Captain Auld "was not born a slaveholder" contribute to the fact that he was so mean?

---

[1] **safe and smoke-house.** A safe is a box where meat is kept. A smoke-house is a small building where meat is preserved by smoke from a slow-burning fire.

[2] **Bay craft.** A boat that is suitable for use in a bay but not on the open sea

[3] **Napoleon.** Napoleon Bonaparte (1770–1837), French emperor and military commander

Vocabulary in Place

destitute, *adj.* Lacking necessary resources or possessions
  The **destitute** children begged for bread in the street.

rigid, *adj.* Inflexible, unyielding
  Wishing to seem less **rigid**, Mrs. Brown excused the class early for recess.

lax, *adj.* Lacking in rigor, not strict
  The principal complained about the **lax** discipline at the pep rallies.

He did nothing of himself. He might have passed for a lion, but for his ears. In all things noble which he attempted, his own meanness shone most conspicuous. His airs, words, and actions, were the airs, words, and actions of born slaveholders, and, being assumed, were awkward enough. He was not even a good imitator. He possessed all the disposition to deceive, but wanted the power. Having no resources within himself, he was compelled to be the copyist of many, and being such, he was forever the victim of inconsistency; and of consequence he was an object of **contempt**, and was held as such even by his slaves. The luxury of having slaves of his own to wait upon him was something new and unprepared for. He was a slaveholder without the ability to hold slaves. He found himself incapable of managing his slaves either by force, fear, or **fraud**. We seldom called him "master;" we generally called him "Captain Auld," and were hardly disposed to title him at all. I doubt not that our conduct had much to do with making him appear awkward, and of consequence **fretful**. Our want of reverence for him must have perplexed him greatly. He wished to have us call him master, but lacked the firmness necessary to command us to do so. His wife used to insist upon our calling him so, but to no purpose. In August, 1832, my master attended a Methodist camp-meeting[4] held in the Bayside, Talbot county, and there experienced religion. I indulged a faint hope that his conversion would lead him to emancipate his

Why was Auld unable to make his slaves call him "master"?

---

[4] **camp-meeting.** A religious gathering, also known as a *revival,* usually hosted by an itinerant, or traveling, preacher

Vocabulary in Place

contempt, *n.* A feeling that something or someone is inferior or worthless; scorn
The drill sergeant had nothing but **contempt** for sloppiness in dress.

fraud, *n.* A deception deliberately practiced to secure unfair or unlawful gain
The bank committed **fraud** by slipping so many unfair, hidden fees into the terms of the loan.

fretful, *adj.* Marked by worry or distress
Maria was kept awake all night by the **fretful** baby.

Illustration entitled "Exhortation and Preaching at the Camp Meeting at Eastham," from *Gleason's Pictorial*, 1852. Library of Congress. LC-USZ62-70638. Used by Permission.

How did religion change Captain Auld as a slave owner?

slaves, and that, if he did not do this, it would, at any rate, make him more kind and humane. I was disappointed in both these respects. It neither made him to be humane to his slaves, nor to emancipate them. If it had any effect on his character, it made him more cruel and hateful in all his ways; for I believe him to have been a much worse man after his conversion than before. Prior to his conversion, he relied upon his own depravity to shield and sustain him in his savage barbarity; but after his conversion, he found religious **sanction** and support for his slaveholding cruelty. He made the greatest **pretensions** to **piety**. His house was the house of prayer. He prayed

---

Vocabulary in Place

sanction, *n.* Authoritative permission or approval
  The doctor would not give **sanction** to the patient's bad habits.

pretension, *n.* A doubtful claim
  We did not trust the salesman despite his **pretensions** to honesty.

piety, *n.* Religious devotion; the desire to perform religious duties
  Some monks express their **piety** by taking a vow of silence.

---

morning, noon, and night. He very soon distinguished himself among his brethren, and was soon made a class-leader and exhorter. His activity in revivals was great, and he proved himself an instrument in the hands of the church in converting many souls. His house was the preachers' home. They used to take great pleasure in coming there to put up; for while he starved us, he stuffed them. We have had three or four preachers there at a time. The names of those who used to come most frequently while I lived there, were Mr. Storks, Mr. Ewery, Mr. Humphry, and Mr. Hickey. I have also seen Mr. George Cookman at our house. We slaves loved Mr. Cookman. We believed him to be a good man. We thought him instrumental in getting Mr. Samuel Harrison, a very rich slaveholder, to emancipate his slaves; and by some means got the impression that he was laboring to effect the emancipation of all the slaves. When he was at our house, we were sure to be called in to prayers. When the others were there, we were sometimes called in and sometimes not. Mr. Cookman took more notice of us than either of the other ministers. He could not come among us without betraying his sympathy for us, and, stupid as we were, we had the **sagacity** to see it.

While I lived with my master in St. Michael's, there was a white young man, a Mr. Wilson, who proposed to keep a Sabbath school for the instruction of such slaves as might be disposed to learn to read the New Testament. We met but three times, when Mr. West and Mr. Fairbanks, both class-leaders, with many others, came upon us with sticks and other missiles, drove us off, and forbade us to meet again. Thus ended our little Sabbath school in the pious town of St. Michael's.

I have said my master found religious sanction for his cruelty. As an example, I will state one of many facts going to prove the charge. I have seen him tie up a lame young woman, and whip her with a heavy cowskin upon her naked shoulders, causing the warm

---

Vocabulary in Place

sagacity, *n.* Soundness of judgment, wisdom
　Citizens rely on the **sagacity** of elected officials in times of crisis.

Why would Captain Auld recite this passage? What does his use of this passage reveal about him?

red blood to drip; and, in justification of the bloody deed, he would quote this passage of Scripture "He that knoweth his master's will, and doeth it not, shall be beaten with many stripes."[5]

Master would keep this lacerated young woman tied up in this horrid situation four or five hours at a time. I have known him to tie her up early in the morning, and whip her before breakfast; leave her, go to his store, return at dinner, and whip her again, cutting her in the places already made raw with his cruel lash. The secret of master's cruelty toward "Henny" is found in the fact of her being almost helpless. When quite a child, she fell into the fire, and burned herself horribly. Her hands were so burnt that she never got the use of them. She could do very little but bear heavy burdens. She was to master a bill of expense; and as he was a mean man, she was a constant offence to him. He seemed desirous of getting the poor girl out of

Why did Auld set Henny "adrift," and what did Douglass think about this?

existence. He gave her away once to his sister; but, being a poor gift, she was not disposed to keep her. Finally, my benevolent master, to use his own words, "set her adrift to take care of herself." Here was a recently-converted man, holding on upon the mother, and at the same time turning out her helpless child, to starve and die! Master Thomas was one of the many pious slaveholders who hold slaves for the very charitable purpose of taking care of them.

My master and myself had quite a number of differences. He found me unsuitable to his purpose. My city life, he said, had had a very **pernicious** effect upon me. It had almost ruined me for every good purpose, and fitted me for every thing which was bad. One of my greatest faults was that of letting his horse run away, and go

How had city life changed Douglass?

---

[5] **He that knoweth . . . shall be beaten with many stripes.**
This quotation from Luke 12:47 refers to Jesus's explanation that the punishment will be stricter for those who know the will of God and fail to follow it than for those who are ignorant. Douglass used it to show how a Biblical passage could be distorted to justify slavery.

Vocabulary in Place

pernicious, *adj.* Destructive
My parents consider television to be a **pernicious** influence and restrict my viewing privileges to one hour per night.

---

down to his father-in-law's farm, which was about five miles from St. Michael's. I would then have to go after it. My reason for this kind of carelessness, or carefulness, was, that I could always get something to eat when I went there. Master William Hamilton, my master's father-in-law, always gave his slaves enough to eat. I never left there hungry, no matter how great the need of my speedy return. Master Thomas at length said he would stand it no longer. I had lived with him nine months, during which time he had given me a number of severe whippings, all to no good purpose. He resolved to put me out, as he said, to be broken; and, for this purpose, he let me for one year to a man named Edward Covey. Mr. Covey was a poor man, a farm-renter. He rented the place upon which he lived, as also the hands with which he tilled it. Mr. Covey had acquired a very high reputation for breaking young slaves, and this reputation was of immense value to him. It enabled him to get his farm tilled with much less expense to himself than he could have had it done without such a reputation. Some slaveholders thought it not much loss to allow Mr. Covey to have their slaves one year, for the sake of the training to which they were subjected, without any other compensation. He could hire young help with great ease, in consequence of this reputation. Added to the natural good qualities of Mr. Covey, he was a professor of religion—a pious soul—a member and a class-leader in the Methodist church. All of this added weight to his reputation as a ". . . breaker." I was aware of all the facts, having been made acquainted with them by a young man who had lived there. I nevertheless made the change gladly; for I was sure of getting enough to eat, which is not the smallest consideration to a hungry man. ▪

What sort of reputation had Covey earned among other slaveholders?

How was Covey different from Auld? Why was Douglass nonetheless glad to go to Covey's?

A racist epithet in the original text has been here deleted.
—The Editors

A Closer Look

Recalling (just the facts)

1. What was considered the meanest practice in slavery, even by slaveholders themselves?

2. Why did Douglass and other enslaved people like Mr. Cookman so much?

3. What was the Sabbath School at St. Michael's?

4. Why was Douglass "loaned" to Covey for a year?

Interpreting (delving deeper)

1. Summarize Auld's personality. Why was he this way, according to Douglass?

2. What effect did religion have on the Aulds? What did Douglass intend to show his readers by describing the Aulds' religious convictions and practices?

3. According to Captain Auld, in what way had city life "ruined" Douglass?

4. Why was Douglass glad to be sent to Covey? Does his attitude surprise you? Explain your answer.

Synthesizing (putting it all together)

The psychologist Abraham Maslow, in a paper written in 1943, proposed that there is a hierarchy of human needs, organized from most to least fundamental, as follows: physiological needs (food and drink, protection from the elements, and so on), safety, love and belonging, self esteem, and self actualization (the need to realize one's full potential). Chapter 9 begins and ends with anecdotes about food and hunger. What makes food (and drink) the most basic of human needs? Why do these needs have to be satisfied before other needs are met? Why was "Not [giving] a slave enough to eat . . . regarded as the most aggravated development of meanness . . . among slaveholders"? ■

Extensions

Writing

A Letter to the Editor. One of the unique elements of a newspaper is the **editorial page**, which features opinion articles written by the editors at the paper and by contributing writers, as well as short letters submitted by readers. These letters provide a platform for people to address important local, state, and national issues.

Imagine that you are an abolitionist living in Douglass's time, around 1850. You have just finished reading a copy of the *Narrative*, which was published just a few years before. Write a letter to the editor of your local newspaper in which you explain why slavery is wrong and should be outlawed in the United States.

The editor of the newspaper has certain guidelines regarding letter submission. First, every letter must be 250 words or less; longer letters will not be published. This requirement will probably limit you to writing two or three paragraphs. In the beginning, however, you should worry only about getting all your ideas on paper. Worry about the word count later.

— Before you start writing, you might want to go to the library or look on the Internet and read letters to the editor in various newspapers.
— Remember to write as if you are living in Douglass's time. Grab your readers' attention, and let them know that there is a great injustice occurring in your society and that it is time to make a change.
— Use specific examples from the *Narrative* to explain why slavery is cruel and unjust. Mention the *Narrative* and its author.
— When you have finished your first draft, count the words (including one-letter words). You may have to go back and cut some parts. Try to do so without weakening your original argument. Keep cutting words and rewriting until you are at or below the word limit. Revise and proofread your letter using the guidelines on pages 170–73. ∎

Extensions

Science

Hunger and Malnutrition. Food is a recurring theme in Douglass's *Narrative.* In Chapter 9, Douglass wrote "Not to give a slave enough to eat, is regarded as the most aggravated development of meanness even among slaveholders. The rule is, no matter how coarse the food, only let there be enough of it." Douglass also described the "painful gnawings of hunger" that he felt during his time with Thomas Auld and the risks that enslaved workers took by stealing or begging from neighbors when slave owners did not provide adequate food.

The need for food is perhaps the most important of the basic human needs; in fact, it is the fundamental driving force behind the actions of all living things. All other needs and wants are soon forgotten by a person (or animal) who has no food.

Your body sends you signals when it wants something to eat. Your stomach aches or "growls." You might feel lightheaded or have trouble concentrating. Most of us experience these signals to some degree during the course of a normal day. Hunger can be a distraction or discomfort, but it can be alleviated easily if you can get your hands on something to eat. However, if you have ever felt hungry but did not have ready access to food, then you probably know that the symptoms get worse, resulting in bodily aches and pains, physical weakness, dizziness, and fatigue.

Persistent hunger—not getting enough to eat day after day—can lead to **malnutrition**, which means that the body has not received essential nutrients. This condition can threaten just about every system and organ in the human body. It should be noted, however, that a lack of food is not the only cause of malnutrition; a person can eat all day long and still be malnourished if he or she is not eating foods that contain the right vitamins, minerals, and other nutrients.

Extensions

Science (cont.)

Young children (under age three) are especially at risk if they do not receive adequate nutrition, but various forms of malnutrition affect people of all ages all over the world. Malnutrition can seriously impair mental and physical health and intellectual development. It can also cause disabilities and lead to premature death.

Below is information from the World Food Program that reveals some of the serious effects of malnutrition.

— Iron deficiency affects nearly two-thirds of the world population and is especially prevalent in **developing countries**, where it impairs the mental development of more than half of all children under four. Foods high in iron include red meats, egg yolks, whole grains, certain beans, and spinach, all of which are hard to come by in places where people live on a dollar a day.

— Iodine deficiency is the greatest single cause of brain damage and mental retardation and affects nearly 1 billion people. Most common table salts that you find in the grocery store are **iodized** for this reason; so, if you live in the United States and other "developed" countries, you should not have to worry about iodine deficiency as long as you get a little salt in your food now and then (iodized salt is used in many of the foods you eat).

— Vitamin A deficiency is another major cause of death and disability. It is the leading cause of childhood blindness in the world. Carrots are among the best sources of Vitamin A. Other sources are spinach, broccoli, and mangoes.

Working in small groups, conduct research in your library or on the Internet to determine some of the other results of malnutrition. Also, identify and research the work of at least one major aid group or international program that is committed to fighting the causes and effects of malnourishment in the world. Present your findings to the class. And eat your spinach! ▪

Chapter 10

PART A

Editorial Note: Chapter 10 of Douglass's *Narrative* is much longer than the other chapters. The editors of this edition have divided the chapter into two parts for ease of treatment in the classroom. The division into two parts is not made in the original text.

Why was Douglass so "awkward" in his new life as a field hand?

I had left Master Thomas's house, and went to live with Mr. Covey, on the 1st of January, 1833. I was now, for the first time in my life, a field hand. In my new employment, I found myself even more awkward than a country boy appeared to be in a large city. I had been at my new home but one week before Mr. Covey gave me a very severe whipping, cutting my back, causing the blood to run, and raising ridges on my flesh as large as my little finger. The details of this affair are as follows: Mr. Covey sent me, very early in the morning of one of our coldest days in the month of January, to the woods, to get a load of wood. He gave me a team of unbroken oxen. He told me which was the in-hand ox, and which the off-hand one.[1] He then tied the end of a large rope around the horns of the in-hand ox, and gave me the other end of it, and told me, if the oxen started to run, that I must hold on upon the rope. I had never driven oxen before, and of course I was very awkward. I, however, succeeded in getting to the edge of the woods with little difficulty; but I had got a very few rods[2] into the woods, when the oxen took fright, and started full tilt, carrying the cart against trees, and over stumps, in the most frightful manner. I expected every moment that my brains would be dashed out against the trees. After running thus for a considerable distance, they finally upset the cart, dashing it with

---

[1] **in-hand . . . off-hand.** The in-hand ox is the lead one. The off-hand ox follows the lead one.

[2] **rod.** A unit of length, approximately sixteen feet. Also, a measuring stick.

great force against a tree, and threw themselves into a dense thicket.[3] How I escaped death, I do not know. There I was, entirely alone, in a thick wood, in a place new to me. My cart was upset and shattered, my oxen were entangled among the young trees, and there was none to help me. After a long spell of effort, I succeeded in getting my cart righted, my oxen disentangled, and again **yoked** to the cart. I now proceeded with my team to the place where I had, the day before, been chopping wood, and loaded my cart pretty heavily, thinking in this way to tame my oxen. I then proceeded on my way home. I had now consumed one half of the day. I got out of the woods safely, and now felt out of danger. I stopped my oxen to open the woods gate; and just as I did so, before I could get hold of my ox-rope, the oxen again started, rushed through the gate, catching it between the wheel and the body of the cart, tearing it to pieces, and coming within a few inches of crushing me against the gate-post. Thus twice, in one short day, I escaped death by the merest chance. On my return, I told Mr. Covey what had happened, and how it happened. He ordered me to return to the woods again immediately. I did so, and he followed on after me. Just as I got into the woods, he came up and told me to stop my cart, and that he would teach me how to **trifle** away my time, and break gates. He then went to a large gum-tree, and with his axe cut three large switches, and, after trimming them up neatly with his pocketknife, he ordered me to take off my clothes. I made him no answer, but stood with my clothes on. He repeated his order. I still made him no answer, nor did I move to strip myself. Upon this he rushed at me with the fierceness of a tiger, tore off my clothes, and

---

[3] **thicket.** A dense growth of shrubs or underbrush

Vocabulary in Place

yoked, *past part.* Joined with a harness
  Before the advent of the tractor, the site of **yoked** oxen pulling a plough was common on farms.

trifle, *v.* To waste
  Roberto **trifled** away his time surfing the Internet when he should have been studying for the test.

lashed me till he had worn out his switches, cutting me so savagely as to leave the marks visible for a long time after. This whipping was the first of a number just like it, and for similar offences.

I lived with Mr. Covey one year. During the first six months, of that year, scarce a week passed without his whipping me. I was seldom free from a sore back. My awkwardness was almost always his excuse for whipping me. We were worked fully up to the point of endurance. Long before day we were up, our horses fed, and by the first approach of day we were off to the field with our hoes and ploughing teams. Mr. Covey gave us enough to eat, but scarce time to eat it. We were often less than five minutes taking our meals. We were often in the field from the first approach of day till its last **lingering** ray had left us; and at saving-fodder time, midnight often caught us in the field binding blades.[4]

Covey would be out with us. The way he used to stand it, was this. He would spend the most of his afternoons in bed. He would then come out fresh in the evening, ready to urge us on with his words, example, and frequently with the whip. Mr. Covey was one of the few slaveholders who could and did work with his hands. He was a hard-working man. He knew by himself just what a man or a boy could do. There was no deceiving him. His work went on in his absence almost as well as in his presence; and he had the faculty of making us feel that he was ever present with us. This he did by surprising us. He seldom approached the spot where we were at work openly, if he could do it secretly. He always aimed at taking us by surprise. Such was his **cunning**, that we used to call him, among

How did Covey make sure that the slaves worked whether or not he was present?

---

[4] **saving-fodder time . . . binding blades.** Fodder is dried grass and other plant stuff used as food for animals. Tall grass would be harvested and its blades bound together for storage and later use as fodder.

Vocabulary in Place

lingering, *part.* Slow in leaving, especially out of reluctance
> She had **lingering** doubts about her choice of colleges.

cunning, *n.* Skill in deception, guile
> Lord Nelson, the British admiral, used **cunning** to defeat the combined French and Spanish fleets at the Battle of Trafalgar.

ourselves, "the snake." When we were at work in the cornfield, he would sometimes crawl on his hands and knees to avoid detection, and all at once he would rise nearly in our midst, and scream out, "Ha, ha! Come, come! Dash on, dash on!" This being his mode of attack, it was never safe to stop a single minute. His comings were like a thief in the night. He appeared to us as being ever at hand. He was under every tree, behind every stump, in every bush, and at every window, on the plantation. He would sometimes mount his horse, as if bound to St. Michael's, a distance of seven miles, and in half an hour afterwards you would see him coiled up in the corner of the wood-fence, watching every motion of the slaves. He would, for this purpose, leave his horse tied up in the woods. Again, he would sometimes walk up to us, and give us orders as though he was upon the point of starting on a long journey, turn his back upon us, and make as though he was going to the house to get ready; and, before he would get half way thither, he would turn short and crawl into a fence-corner, or behind some tree, and there watch us till the going down of the sun.

Mr. Covey's **forte** consisted in his power to deceive. His life was devoted to planning and perpetrating the grossest deceptions. Every thing he possessed in the shape of learning or religion, he made conform to his disposition to deceive. He seemed to think himself equal to deceiving the Almighty. He would make a short prayer in the morning, and a long prayer at night; and, strange as it may seem, few men would at times appear more devotional than he. The exercises of his family devotions were always commenced with singing; and, as he was a very poor singer himself, the duty of raising the hymn generally came upon me. He would read his hymn,

---

Vocabulary in Place

forte, *n.* Something in which a person excels. When used in this sense, the word is pronounced with a silent final *e:* /fort/.

Since persuasive argumentation was his **forte,** Sam was chosen to be captain of our debate team.

---

and nod at me to commence. I would at times do so; at others, I would not. My non-compliance would almost always produce much confusion. To show himself independent of me, he would start and stagger through with his hymn in the most discordant manner. In this state of mind, he prayed with more than ordinary spirit. Poor man! such was his disposition, and success at deceiving, I do verily believe that he sometimes deceived himself into the solemn belief, that he was a sincere worshipper of the most high God; and this, too, at a time when he may be said to have been guilty of compelling his woman slave to commit the sin of adultery. The facts in the case are these: Mr. Covey was a poor man; he was just commencing in life; he was only able to buy one slave; and, shocking as is the fact, he bought her, as he said, for A BREEDER. This woman was named Caroline. Mr. Covey bought her from Mr. Thomas Lowe, about six miles from St. Michael's. She was a large, able-bodied woman, about twenty years old. She had already given birth to one child, which proved her to be just what he wanted. After buying her, he hired a married man of Mr. Samuel Harrison, to live with him one year; and him he used to fasten up with her every night! The result was, that, at the end of the year, the miserable woman gave birth to twins. At this result Mr. Covey seemed to be highly pleased, both with the man and the wretched woman. Such was his joy, and that of his wife, that nothing they could do for Caroline during her confinement was too good, or too hard, to be done. The children were regarded as being quite an addition to his wealth.

How does this passage show that enslaved people were given the same treatment or status as ordinary livestock?

If at any one time of my life more than another, I was made to drink the bitterest **dregs** of slavery, that time was during the first six months of my stay with Mr. Covey. We were worked in all weathers. It was never too hot or too cold; it could never rain, blow, hail, or snow, too hard for us to work in the field. Work, work, work, was scarcely more the order of the day than of the night. The longest

Vocabulary in Place
dregs, *n.* The bottom part of a liquid, containing sediment that has settled; the least desirable portion   Please make a new pot of tea; there's nothing left but the **dregs**.

days were too short for him, and the shortest nights too long for him. I was somewhat unmanageable when I first went there, but a few months of this discipline tamed me. Mr. Covey succeeded in breaking me. I was broken in body, soul, and spirit. My natural elasticity was crushed, my intellect **languished**, the disposition to read departed, the cheerful spark that lingered about my eye died; the dark night of slavery closed in upon me; and behold a man transformed into a brute!

How and why did Douglass change during the first few months with Covey?

Sunday was my only leisure time. I spent this in a sort of beast-like **stupor**, between sleep and wake, under some large tree. At times I would rise up, a flash of energetic freedom would dart through my soul, accompanied with a faint beam of hope, that flickered for a moment, and then vanished. I sank down again, mourning over my wretched condition. I was sometimes prompted to take my life, and that of Covey, but was prevented by a combination of hope and fear. My sufferings on this plantation seem now like a dream rather than a stern reality.

Our house stood within a few rods of the Chesapeake Bay, whose broad bosom was ever white with sails from every quarter of the habitable globe. Those beautiful vessels, robed in purest white, so delightful to the eye of freemen, were to me so many shrouded ghosts, to terrify and torment me with thoughts of my wretched condition. I have often, in the deep stillness of a summer's Sabbath, stood all alone upon the **lofty** banks of that noble bay, and traced, with saddened heart and tearful eye, the countless number of sails moving off to the mighty ocean. The sight of these always affected me powerfully. My thoughts would compel utterance; and there, with no audience but

Did the sight of the ships make Douglass feel happy or sad? Why?

Vocabulary in Place

languish, *v.* To become weak or feeble; lose strength
   It is better to live an active life than to **languish** in front of the television set.

stupor, *n.* A state of greatly decreased sensibility or physical activity
   For several minutes after the accident, Bill was in a **stupor**.

lofty, *adj.* Of great height, elevated, exalted
   Distracted by his **lofty** thoughts, Bob tripped on his way down the stairs.

Narrative of the Life of Frederick Douglass   *107*

the Almighty, I would pour out my soul's complaint, in my rude way, with an **apostrophe** to the moving multitude of ships:—

"You are loosed from your moorings, and are free; I am fast in my chains, and am a slave! You move merrily before the gentle gale, and I sadly before the bloody whip! You are freedom's swift-winged angels, that fly round the world; I am confined in bands of iron! O that I were free! O, that I were on one of your **gallant** decks, and under your protecting wing! Alas! betwixt me and you, the **turbid** waters roll. Go on, go on. O that I could also go! Could I but swim! If I could fly! O, why was I born a man, of whom to make a brute! The glad ship is gone; she hides in the dim distance. I am left in the hottest hell of unending slavery. O God, save me! God, deliver me! Let me be free! Is there any God? Why am I a slave? I will run away.

"Entering Harbor." Painting by Francis Davis Millet, ca.1900. Library of Congress, Company Collection, reproduction number LC-D416-429. Used by Permission.

Vocabulary in Place

apostrophe, *n.* A literary device in which a nonhuman thing is addressed directly, as though it were a person

> A famous example of an **apostrophe** is Shelley's poem "Ode to the West Wind."

gallant, *adj.* Valiant or unflinching in action or battle

> The **gallant** firefighters rushed without hesitation into the burning building.

turbid, *adj.* Lacking clarity, foul, muddy

> One could barely see the large catfish moving in the depths of the **turbid** water.

I will not stand it. Get caught, or get clear, I'll try it. I had as well die with ague as the fever. I have only one life to lose. I had as well be killed running as die standing. Only think of it; one hundred miles straight north, and I am free! Try it? Yes! God helping me, I will. It cannot be that I shall live and die a slave. I will take to the water. This very bay shall yet bear me into freedom. The steamboats steered in a north-east course from North Point. I will do the same; and when I get to the head of the bay, I will turn my canoe adrift, and walk straight through Delaware into Pennsylvania. When I get there, I shall not be required to have a pass; I can travel without being disturbed. Let but the first opportunity offer, and, come what will, I am off. Meanwhile, I will try to bear up under the yoke. I am not the only slave in the world. Why should I fret? I can bear as much as any of them. Besides, I am but a boy, and all boys are bound to some one. It may be that my misery in slavery will only increase my happiness when I get free. There is a better day coming."

Thus I used to think, and thus I used to speak to myself; goaded almost to madness at one moment, and at the next reconciling myself to my wretched lot.

I have already intimated that my condition was much worse, during the first six months of my stay at Mr. Covey's, than in the last six. The circumstances leading to the change in Mr. Covey's course toward me form an epoch in my humble history.[5] You have seen how a man was made a slave; you shall see how a slave was made a man. On one of the hottest days of the month of August, 1833, Bill Smith, William Hughes, a slave named Eli, and myself, were engaged in fanning wheat.[6] Hughes was clearing the fanned wheat from before the fan. Eli was turning, Smith was feeding, and I was carrying wheat to the fan. The work was simple, requiring strength rather than intellect; yet, to one entirely unused to such work, it came very hard. About three o'clock of that day, I broke down; my strength failed me; I was seized with a violent aching of the head, attended with extreme

---

[5] **an epoch in my humble history.** An important period in his life

[6] **fanning wheat.** Threshing the wheat, or beating it to separate the edible grain from the inedible chaff

dizziness; I trembled in every limb. Finding what was coming, I nerved myself up, feeling it would never do to stop work. I stood as long as I could stagger to the hopper with grain. When I could stand no longer, I fell, and felt as if held down by an immense weight. The fan of course stopped; every one had his own work to do; and no one could do the work of the other, and have his own go on at the same time.

Mr. Covey was at the house, about one hundred yards from the treading-yard where we were fanning. On hearing the fan stop, he left immediately, and came to the spot where we were. He hastily inquired what the matter was. Bill answered that I was sick, and there was no one to bring wheat to the fan. I had by this time crawled away under the side of the post and rail-fence by which the yard was enclosed, hoping to find relief by getting out of the sun. He then asked where I was. He was told by one of the hands. He came to the spot, and, after looking at me awhile, asked me what was the matter. I told him as well as I could, for I scarce had strength to speak. He then gave me a savage kick in the side, and told me to get up. I tried to do so, but fell back in the attempt. He gave me another kick, and again told me to rise. I again tried, and succeeded in gaining my feet; but, stooping to get the tub with which I was feeding the fan, I again staggered and fell. While down in this situation, Mr. Covey took up the hickory slat with which Hughes had been striking off the half-bushel measure, and with it gave me a heavy blow upon the head, making a large wound, and the blood ran freely; and with this again told me to get up. I made no effort to **comply**, having now made up my mind to let him do his worst. In a short time after receiving this blow, my head grew better. Mr. Covey had now left me to my fate. At this moment I resolved, for the first time, to go to my master, enter a complaint, and ask his protection. In order to do this, I must that afternoon walk seven miles; and this, under the

Where did Douglass plan to go after Covey beat him, and what did he intend to do?

Vocabulary in Place

comply, v. To act in accordance with another's command or request
   "Please **comply** with all lighted signs and placards," said the flight attendant, pointing to the "fasten seatbelts" sign.

circumstances, was truly a severe undertaking. I was exceedingly **feeble**; made so as much by the kicks and blows which I received, as by the severe fit of sickness to which I had been subjected. I, however, watched my chance, while Covey was looking in an opposite direction, and started for St. Michael's. I succeeded in getting a considerable distance on my way to the woods, when Covey discovered me, and called after me to come back, threatening what he would do if I did not come. I disregarded both his calls and his threats, and made my way to the woods as fast as my feeble state would allow; and thinking I might be over-hauled by him if I kept the road, I walked through the woods, keeping far enough from the road to avoid detection, and near enough to prevent losing my way. I had not gone far before my little strength again failed me. I could go no farther. I fell down, and lay for a considerable time. The blood was yet oozing from the wound on my head. For a time I thought I should bleed to death; and think now that I should have done so, but that the blood so matted my hair as to stop the wound. After lying there about three quarters of an hour, I nerved myself up again, and started on my way, through bogs and briers, barefooted and bareheaded, tearing my feet sometimes at nearly every step; and after a journey of about seven miles, occupying some five hours to perform it, I arrived at master's store. I then presented an appearance enough to affect any but a heart of iron. From the crown of my head to my feet, I was covered with blood. My hair was all clotted with dust and blood; my shirt was stiff with blood. I suppose I looked like a man who had escaped a den of wild beasts, and barely escaped them. In this state I appeared before my master, humbly entreating him to interpose his authority for my protection. I told him all the circumstances as well as I could, and it seemed, as I spoke, at times to affect him. He would then walk the floor, and seek to justify Covey by saying he expected

---

Vocabulary in Place

feeble, *adj.* Lacking strength, weak
Her defense seemed **feeble** in light of all the evidence against her.

Did Master Thomas help Douglass? What did he tell Douglass to do? Why?

I deserved it. He asked me what I wanted. I told him, to let me get a new home; that as sure as I lived with Mr. Covey again, I should live with but to die with him; that Covey would surely kill me; he was in a fair way for it. Master Thomas ridiculed the idea that there was any danger of Mr. Covey's killing me, and said that he knew Mr. Covey; that he was a good man, and that he could not think of taking me from him; that, should he do so, he would lose the whole year's wages; that I belonged to Mr. Covey for one year, and that I must go back to him, come what might; and that I must not trouble him with any more stories, or that he would himself GET HOLD OF ME. After threatening me thus, he gave me a very large dose of salts, telling me that I might remain in St. Michael's that night (it being quite late) but that I must be off back to Mr. Covey's early in the morning; and that if I did not, he would GET HOLD OF ME, which meant that he would whip me. I remained all night, and, according to his orders, I started off to Covey's in the morning, (Saturday morning,) wearied in body and broken in spirit. I got no supper that night, or breakfast that morning. I reached Covey's about nine o'clock; and just as I was getting over the fence that divided Mrs. Kemp's fields from ours, out ran Covey with his cowskin, to give me another whipping. Before he could reach me, I succeeded in getting to the cornfield; and as the corn was very high, it afforded me the means of hiding. He seemed very angry, and searched for me a long time. My behavior was altogether unaccountable. He finally gave up the chase, thinking, I suppose, that I must come home for something to eat; he would give himself no further trouble in looking for me. I spent that day mostly in the woods, having the alternative before me,—to go home and be whipped to death, or stay in the woods and be starved to death. That night, I fell in with Sandy Jenkins, a slave with whom I was somewhat acquainted. Sandy had a free wife who lived about four miles from Mr. Covey's; and it being Saturday, he was on his way to see her. I told him my circumstances, and he very kindly invited me to go home with him. I went home with him, and talked this whole matter over, and got his advice as to what course it was best for me to pursue. I found Sandy an old adviser. He told me, with great solemnity, I must go back to Covey; but that before I

Who was Sandy Jenkins? Why did Douglass trust his advice?

112

Illustration entitled "Found in the Woods by Sandy" from *Frederick Douglass, My Bondage and My Freedom.* New York: Miller, Orton and Mulligan, ca.1855. Special Collections, University of Virginia. Used by Permission.

went, I must go with him into another part of the woods, where there was a certain ROOT, which, if I would take some of it with me, carrying it ALWAYS ON MY RIGHT SIDE, would render it impossible for Mr. Covey, or any other white man, to whip me. He said he had carried it for years; and since he had done so, he had never received a blow, and never expected to while he carried it. I at first rejected the idea, that the simple carrying of a root in my pocket would have any such effect as he had said, and was not disposed to take it; but Sandy impressed the necessity with much earnestness, telling me it could do no harm, if it did no good. To please him, I at length took the root, and, according to his direction, carried it upon my right side. This was Sunday morning. I immediately started for home; and upon entering the yard gate, out came Mr. Covey on his way to meeting. He spoke to me very kindly, bade me drive the pigs from a lot near by, and passed on towards the church. Now, this **singular** conduct of Mr. Covey really made me begin to think that there was something in the ROOT which Sandy had given me; and had it been on any other day than Sunday, I could have attributed the conduct to no other cause than the influence of that root; and as it was, I was half inclined to think the ROOT to be something more than I at first had taken it to be. All went well till Monday morning. On this morning, the virtue of the ROOT was fully tested. Long before daylight, I was called to go and rub, curry,[7] and feed, the horses. I obeyed, and was glad to obey. But whilst thus engaged, whilst in the act of throwing down some blades from the loft, Mr. Covey entered the stable with a long rope; and just as I was half out of the loft, he caught hold of my legs, and was about tying me. As soon as I found what he was up to, I gave a sudden spring, and as I did so, he holding to my legs, I was brought sprawling on the stable floor. Mr. Covey seemed now to think he had me, and could do what

---

[7] **curry.** To groom with a special comb

> **Vocabulary in Place**
>
> **singular,** *adj.* Unusual or remarkable, unique
> The belly-pouch is a **singular** characteristic of kangaroos and other marsupials.

he pleased; but at this moment—from whence came the spirit I don't know—I resolved to fight; and, suiting my action to the resolution, I seized Covey hard by the throat; and as I did so, I rose. He held on to me, and I to him. My resistance was so entirely unexpected that Covey seemed taken all aback. He trembled like a leaf. This gave me assurance, and I held him uneasy, causing the blood to run where I touched him with the ends of my fingers. Mr. Covey soon called out to Hughes for help. Hughes came, and, while Covey held me, attempted to tie my right hand. While he was in the act of doing so, I watched my chance, and gave him a heavy kick close under the ribs. This kick fairly sickened Hughes, so that he left me in the hands of Mr. Covey. This kick had the effect of not only weakening Hughes, but Covey also. When he saw Hughes bending over with pain, his courage **quailed**. He asked me if I meant to persist in my resistance. I told him I did, come what might; that he had used me like a brute for six months, and that I was determined to be used so no longer. With that, he strove to drag me to a stick that was lying just out of the stable door. He meant to knock me down. But just as he was leaning over to get the stick, I seized him with both hands by his collar, and brought him by a sudden snatch to the ground. By this time, Bill came. Covey called upon him for assistance. Bill wanted to know what he could do. Covey said, "Take hold of him, take hold of him!" Bill said his master hired him out to work, and not to help to whip me; so he left Covey and myself to fight our own battle out. We were at it for nearly two hours. Covey at length let me go, puffing and blowing at a great rate, saying that if I had not resisted, he would not have whipped me half so much. The truth was, that he had not whipped me at all. I considered him as getting entirely the worst end of the bargain; for he had drawn no blood from me, but I had from him. The whole six months afterwards, that I spent with Mr. Covey, he never laid the weight of his finger upon me in anger. He would occasionally

Why did Covey lose his courage when Douglass kicked Mr. Hughes?

Vocabulary in Place

quail, v. To flinch, give way, or falter
   My dog always **quails** at the first hint of thunder.

---

say, he didn't want to get hold of me again. "No," thought I, "you need not; for you will come off worse than you did before."

This battle with Mr. Covey was the turning point in my career as a slave. It rekindled the few expiring embers of freedom, and revived within me a sense of my own manhood. It recalled the departed self-confidence, and inspired me again with a determination to be free. The gratification afforded by the triumph was a full compensation for whatever else might follow, even death itself. He only can understand the deep satisfaction which I experienced, who has himself repelled by force the bloody arm of slavery. I felt as I never felt before. It was a glorious resurrection, from the tomb of slavery, to the heaven of freedom. My long-crushed spirit rose, cowardice departed, bold **defiance** took its place; and I now resolved that, however long I might remain a slave in form, the day had passed forever when I could be a slave in fact. I did not hesitate to let it be known of me, that the white man who expected to succeed in whipping, must also succeed in killing me.

From this time I was never again what might be called fairly whipped, though I remained a slave four years afterwards. I had several fights, but was never whipped.

It was for a long time a matter of surprise to me why Mr. Covey did not immediately have me taken by the constable[8] to the whipping-post, and there regularly whipped for the crime of raising my hand against a white man in defence of myself. And the only explanation I can now think of does not entirely satisfy me; but such as it is, I will give it. Mr. Covey enjoyed the most unbounded reputation for being a first-rate overseer and negro-breaker. It was of considerable importance to him. That reputation was at stake; and had he sent me—a boy about sixteen years old—to the public whipping-post, his reputation would have been lost; so, to save his reputation, he suffered me to go unpunished.

> What did Douglass mean when he said "however long I might remain a slave in form, the day had passed forever when I could be a slave in fact"?

---

[8] **constable.** A peace officer with less power or authority than a sheriff

Vocabulary in Place

defiance, *n.* Bold resistance, opposition to authority
  Rosa Parks' refusal to move to the back of the bus was a famous act of **defiance.**

116

A Closer Look

Recalling (just the facts)

1. Why did slaves call Covey "the snake"?

2. What did Douglass see when he looked out on the Chesapeake Bay?

3. What did Sandy Jenkins give Douglass for protection? What was Douglass supposed to do with this item?

4. What event marked the turning point in Douglass's "career" as a slave?

Interpreting (delving deeper)

1. What was Covey's reason for trying to deceive the slaves? What effect did his deceptions have on Douglass and the others?

2. At the end of his apostrophe to the ships, Douglass said, "It may be that my misery in slavery will only increase my happiness when I get free." What did he mean?

3. Would Sandy Jenkins say that the root worked for Douglass? To what would Douglass probably attribute the fact that he was never beaten again?

4. What did Douglass mean when he said that "the white man who expected to succeed in whipping, must also succeed in killing me"?

Synthesizing (putting it all together)

"You have seen how a man was made a slave; you shall see how a slave was made a man." Discuss the importance of this quotation from Chapter 10, Part A. ▪

Extensions

The Apostrophe. Have you ever wished that you could soar above the earth like a bird or swim to the depths of the ocean like a whale? Eventually in life, everyone has a desire to do something that is simply impossible or wishes that he or she could be with someone who is absent. Poets, playwrights, and other writers have a tool to help them deal with such desires—the apostrophe.

An **apostrophe** is an address or speech either to an absent person or to an inanimate object such as a tree or a cloud. When the object of an apostrophe is inanimate, that object is **personified**, meaning that the writer speaks to it as if it had the senses and intellect of a human being. An apostrophe can express any emotion, though most often an apostrophe is used to convey frustration, grief, or a desire for something that is beyond reach. Birds, stars, oceans, and mountains are commonly addressed in apostrophic form by poets and songwriters.

Douglass calls his own apostrophe "rude," but it is not rude, or simple, at all. It is justly famous for its powerful imagery and language contrasting the bonds of slavery with the freedom enjoyed by sailors on the Chesapeake Bay.

Try your hand at writing your own apostrophe. You may choose to address an inanimate object, as did the poet Lord Byron in his "Apostrophe to the Ocean" (from a longer poem called *Childe Harold's Pilgrimage)* or the poet Pablo Neruda in his "Ode to My Socks." Or, you may choose to address an absent person, such as an ancestor or a famous historical figure.

—You may write a poem or simply write in prose form, as Douglass did.

—You must write using the second-person narrative form, addressing the object or absent person directly.

Extensions

Writing (cont.)

—An apostrophe can be serious, like Douglass's apostrophe in Chapter 10, or it can be light-hearted and amusing, like Neruda's "Ode to My Socks." You can write either kind of apostrophe.

—Traditionally, apostrophes contain exalted, dramatic language. Let your imagination and emotions flow in your writing.

—If you decide to write a light-hearted, comic apostrophe, try using flowery, exalted language to speak about your humble subject. The contrast between a silly or light-hearted subject and very serious, very formal language can be amusing.

—Here are some possible subjects to choose from. Choose one of these or a subject of your own:

> For a serious apostrophe: to friendship; to the Lincoln Memorial; to Thomas Jefferson or Martin Luther King, Jr.; to my ancestors; to my children as yet unborn
>
> For a comic apostrophe: to my skateboard; to my old tennis shoes; to a broken guitar string; to a blackboard; to a plate of French Fries

—Choose an emotion, or **mood**, that you want to convey in your apostrophe, such as sadness, anger, joy, silliness, wistfulness, regret, hope, or sarcasm. Choose your language and details to convey that emotion.

—After you have chosen your subject and the emotion that you want to convey, do some brainstorming of ideas to use in your piece. You may want to make a word web, or cluster chart. Write your main topic in the middle of a piece of blank paper and circle it. Think of related ideas and write these outside the circled main topic. Circle the related ideas. Then draw lines to connect the ideas.

Extensions

Folk Medicine.

I found Sandy an old adviser. He told me, with great solemnity, I must go back to Covey; but that before I went, I must go with him into another part of the woods, where there was a certain ROOT, which, if I would take some of it with me, carrying it ALWAYS ON MY RIGHT SIDE, would render it impossible for Mr. Covey, or any other white man, to whip me. He said he had carried it for years; and since he had done so, he had never received a blow, and never expected to while he carried it. I at first rejected the idea, that the simple carrying of a root in my pocket would have any such effect as he had said, and was not disposed to take it; but Sandy impressed the necessity with much earnestness, telling me it could do no harm, if it did no good. To please him, I at length took the root, and, according to his direction, carried it upon my right side.

Frederick Douglass did not think it strange or surprising when Sandy Jenkins gave him a special root to protect him from the slave owner's cruelty. In fact, the use of roots and herbs for medicinal and protective purposes was part of daily life for slaves in the southern United States. Such practices are often referred to as **folk medicine** because they involve knowledge that has been passed down orally through the generations.

In many African cultures, certain tasks, often cooking, making cloth, sewing, midwifery, and healing, were deemed "women's work." These customs and societal structures were not forgotten. On southern plantations, especially in remote areas where doctors (practitioners of Western medicine) were rare, enslaved women were relied upon as healers and midwives. These women earned special status, and often were called in to treat the slaveholder's family as well as the slaves. Douglass's grandmother probably served in this capacity (see Chapter 8). He wrote, of her service to his old master, that "She had rocked him in infancy, attended him in childhood,

Extensions

served him through life, and at his death wiped from his icy brow the cold death-sweat." Douglass did not specifically mention any folk medicine, but it is probable that this "great" grandmother had broad knowledge of herbal remedies.

The healers' knowledge was rooted in African traditions, though they had to adapt their practices to the types of plants available in a given region. Their methods were typically a mix of "real" medicine and magic or superstition. For instance, teas and powders made from the herb *St. John's Wort* are still prescribed by doctors today (especially in Europe) to treat depression, digestive problems, and other maladies. Poultice (paste) made from the plant is also used to treat burns and ulcers. On the other hand, some healers believed that *St. John's Wort* caused evil spirits to flee in panic. Was Sandy Jenkins's root used for medicinal or "magical" purposes?

Healers with the best reputations were sometimes hired out to other plantations and paid for their services, and some records indicate that women were able to earn their freedom in exchange for divulging the secrets of their trade. Theirs was not a guessing game; nothing was done by trial and error. Rather, the healers relied on inherited knowledge of the medicinal value of herbs in the surrounding forests and fields.

A simple tea made from any number of plants in the mint family (peppermint, spearmint, catnip) was used to calm the nerves, to quiet fussy babies, and to ease digestive problems. Teas made from red oak bark could cure **dysentery**, a potentially deadly disease caused by bacteria in water or food. Parts of the paradise tree and the senna plant were used to expel intestinal worms. Pine **rosin** (sap) was used to protect and sooth various wounds. A few of the other herbs and roots referred to in slave narratives and other primary source material are pennyroyal, snake root, cherry bark, ginseng, dogwood, horehound, and sarsaparilla.

Extensions

It should be noted that abuse or misuse of any wild plant can be extremely dangerous, even deadly, and nobody without a high level of medical training or the guidance of an expert should attempt to administer herbal remedies.

Conduct research into medicinal plants and traditional practices associated with these plants, including the way they might have been used by African or Native Americans. Internet research tip: look up the term <u>traditional medicine</u> in combination with one of the following:

—aspirin (from the willow tree)

—digitalis (from fox glove)

—quinine (from the chinchona tree)

—morphine (from the poppy flower)

—vincristine and vinblastine (from the rosy periwinkle) ▪

Chapter 10

PART B

My term of actual service to Mr. Edward Covey ended on Christmas day, 1833. The days between Christmas and New Year's Day are allowed as holidays; and, accordingly, we were not required to perform any labor, more than to feed and take care of the stock. This time we regarded as our own, by the grace of our masters; and we therefore used or abused it nearly as we pleased. Those of us who had families at a distance, were generally allowed to spend the whole six days in their society. This time, however, was spent in various ways. The **staid**, sober, thinking and industrious ones of our number would employ themselves in making corn-brooms, mats, horse-collars, and baskets; and another class of us would spend the time in hunting opossums, hares, and coons.[1] But by far the larger part engaged in such sports and merriments as playing ball, wrestling, running foot-races, fiddling, dancing, and drinking whisky; and this latter mode of spending the time was by far the most agreeable to the feelings of our masters. A slave who would work during the holidays was considered by our masters as scarcely deserving them. He was regarded as one who rejected the favor of his master. It was deemed a disgrace not to get drunk at Christmas; and he was regarded as lazy indeed, who had not provided himself with

Editorial Note: Chapter 10 of Douglass's *Narrative* is much longer than the other chapters. The editors of this edition have divided the chapter into two parts for ease of treatment in the classroom. The division into parts is not made in the original text.

---

[1]**hares, and coons.** Rabbits and raccoons

Vocabulary in Place
staid, *adj.* Serious, sober, marked by self-restraint June is so **staid** that she often seems older than she really is.

the necessary means, during the year, to get whisky enough to last him through Christmas.

From what I know of the effect of these holidays upon the slave, I believe them to be among the most effective means in the hands of the slaveholder in keeping down the spirit of **insurrection**. Were the slaveholders at once to abandon this practice, I have not the slightest doubt it would lead to an immediate insurrection among the slaves. These holidays serve as conductors, or safety-valves, to carry off the rebellious spirit of enslaved humanity. But for these, the slave would be forced up to the wildest desperation; and woe betide the slaveholder, the day he ventures to remove or hinder the operation of those conductors! I warn him that, in such an event, a spirit will go forth in their midst, more to be dreaded than the most appalling earthquake.

The holidays are part and parcel of the gross fraud, wrong, and inhumanity of slavery. They are professedly a custom established by the **benevolence** of the slaveholders; but I undertake to say, it is the result of selfishness, and one of the grossest frauds committed upon the down-trodden slave. They do not give the slaves this time because they would not like to have their work during its continuance, but because they know it would be unsafe to deprive them of it. This will be seen by the fact that the slaveholders like to have their slaves spend those days just in such a manner as to make them as glad of their ending as of their beginning. Their object seems to be, to disgust their slaves with freedom, by plunging them into the lowest depths of dissipation. For instance, the slaveholders not only like to see the slave drink of his own accord, but will adopt various plans to make him drunk. One plan is, to make bets on their slaves, as to who can drink the most whisky without getting drunk; and in this way they succeed in getting whole multitudes to drink to

---

Vocabulary in Place

insurrection, *n.* Open revolt against civil authority
Slave owners lived in fear of an **insurrection** mounted by their slaves.

benevolence, *n.* Kindness
Andrew Carnegie showed certain **benevolence** through his gifts of public libraries to American communities.

excess. Thus, when the slave asks for virtuous freedom, the cunning slaveholder, knowing his ignorance, cheats him with a dose of vicious dissipation, artfully labeled with the name of liberty. The most of us used to drink it down, and the result was just what might be supposed; many of us were led to think that there was little to choose between liberty and slavery. We felt, and very properly too, that we had almost as well be slaves to man as to rum. So, when the holidays ended, we staggered up from the filth of our wallowing, took a long breath, and marched to the field,—feeling, upon the whole, rather glad to go, from what our master had deceived us into a belief was freedom, back to the arms of slavery.

I have said that this mode of treatment is a part of the whole system of fraud and inhumanity of slavery. It is so. The mode here adopted to disgust the slave with freedom, by allowing him to see only the abuse of it, is carried out in other things. For instance, a slave loves molasses; he steals some. His master, in many cases, goes off to town, and buys a large quantity; he returns, takes his whip, and commands the slave to eat the molasses, until the poor fellow is made sick at the very mention of it. The same mode is sometimes adopted to make the slaves refrain from asking for more food than their regular allowance. A slave runs through his allowance, and applies for more. His master is enraged at him; but, not willing to send him off without food, gives him more than is necessary, and compels him to eat it within a given time. Then, if he complains that he cannot eat it, he is said to be satisfied neither full nor fasting, and is whipped for being hard to please! I have an abundance of such illustrations of the same principle, drawn from my own observation, but think the cases I have cited sufficient. The practice is a very common one.

On the first of January, 1834, I left Mr. Covey, and went to live with Mr. William Freeland, who lived about three miles from St. Michael's. I soon found Mr. Freeland a very different man from Mr. Covey. Though not rich, he was what would be called an educated southern gentleman. Mr. Covey, as I have shown, was a well-trained negro-breaker and slave-driver. The former (slaveholder though he was) seemed to possess some regard for honor, some reverence for justice, and some respect for humanity. The latter seemed totally

What did Douglass mean when he said that the holidays were intended to "disgust the slave with freedom"?

Were Mr. Freeland and Mr. Covey very different in terms of the ways in which they treated the enslaved?

insensible to all such sentiments. Mr. Freeland had many of the faults peculiar to slaveholders, such as being very passionate and fretful; but I must do him the justice to say that he was exceedingly free from those degrading vices to which Mr. Covey was constantly addicted. The one was open and frank, and we always knew where to find him. The other was a most artful deceiver, and could be understood only by such as were skilful enough to detect his cunningly-devised frauds. Another advantage I gained in my new master was, he made no pretensions to, or profession of, religion; and this, in my opinion, was truly a great advantage. I assert most unhesitatingly, that the religion of the south is a mere covering for the most horrid crimes,—a justifier of the most appalling barbarity,—a sanctifier of the most hateful frauds,—and a dark shelter under which the

Why did Douglass consider it a "calamity" to be the property of a religious slaveholder?

darkest, foulest, grossest, and most infernal deeds of slaveholders find the strongest protection. Were I to be again reduced to the chains of slavery, next to that enslavement, I should regard being the slave of a religious master the greatest **calamity** that could befall me. For of all slaveholders with whom I have ever met, religious slaveholders are the worst. I have ever found them the meanest and basest, the most cruel and cowardly, of all others. It was my unhappy lot not only to belong to a religious slaveholder, but to live in a community of such religionists. Very near Mr. Freeland lived the Rev. Daniel Weeden, and in the same neighborhood lived the Rev. Rigby Hopkins. These were members and ministers in the Reformed Methodist Church.[2] Mr. Weeden owned, among others, a woman slave, whose name I have forgotten. This woman's back, for weeks, was kept literally raw,

Did Mr. Weeden whip his slaves regardless of how they had behaved?

made so by the lash of this merciless, RELIGIOUS wretch. He used to hire hands. His maxim was, Behave well or behave ill, it is the

---

[2] **Reformed Methodist Church.** One of many denominations to arise during the first half of the nineteenth century as a result of disagreements among members of the American Methodist Church

Vocabulary in Place
calamity, *n.* An extraordinary disaster causing great loss or grief The loss of its treasure fleet due to a hurricane in 1715 was a **calamity** from which the Spanish empire never fully recovered.

duty of a master occasionally to whip a slave, to remind him of his master's authority. Such was his theory, and such his practice.

Mr. Hopkins was even worse than Mr. Weeden. His chief boast was his ability to manage slaves. The peculiar feature of his government was that of whipping slaves in advance of deserving it. He always managed to have one or more of his slaves to whip every Monday morning. He did this to alarm their fears, and strike terror into those who escaped. His plan was to whip for the smallest offences, to prevent the commission of large ones. Mr. Hopkins could always find some excuse for whipping a slave. It would astonish one, unaccustomed to a slave-holding life, to see with what wonderful ease a slave-holder can find things, of which to make occasion to whip a slave. A mere look, word, or motion,—a mistake, accident, or want of power,—are all matters for which a slave may be whipped at any time. Does a slave look dissatisfied? It is said, he has the devil in him, and it must be whipped out. Does he speak loudly when spoken to by his master? Then he is getting high-minded, and should be taken down a button-hole lower. Does he forget to pull off his hat at the approach of a white person? Then he is wanting in reverence, and should be whipped for it. Does he ever venture to **vindicate** his conduct, when censured for it? Then he is guilty of impudence,—one of the greatest crimes of which a slave can be guilty. Does he ever venture to suggest a different mode of doing things from that pointed out by his master? He is indeed presumptuous, and getting above himself; and nothing less than a flogging will do for him. Does he, while ploughing, break a plough,—or, while hoeing, break a hoe? It is owing to his carelessness, and for it a slave must always be whipped. Mr. Hopkins could always find something of this sort to justify the use of the lash, and he seldom failed to embrace such opportunities. There was not a man in the whole county, with whom the slaves who had the getting their own home, would not prefer to

Why did Mr. Hopkins whip slaves "in advance of deserving it"?

Vocabulary in Place

vindicate, *v.* To justify, to clear of blame, or to prove the worth of
The lawyer found new evidence to **vindicate** his client.

---

live, rather than with this Rev. Mr. Hopkins. And yet there was not a man any where round, who made higher professions of religion, or was more active in revivals,—more attentive to the class, love-feast, prayer and preaching meetings, or more devotional in his family,—that prayed earlier, later, louder, and longer,—than this same reverend slave-driver, Rigby Hopkins.

But to return to Mr. Freeland, and to my experience while in his employment. He, like Mr. Covey, gave us enough to eat; but, unlike Mr. Covey, he also gave us sufficient time to take our meals. He worked us hard, but always between sunrise and sunset. He required a good deal of work to be done, but gave us good tools with which to work. His farm was large, but he employed hands enough to work it, and with ease, compared with many of his neighbors. My treatment, while in his employment, was heavenly, compared with what I experienced at the hands of Mr. Edward Covey.

Was Douglass enslaved by Mr. Freeland?

Mr. Freeland was himself the owner of but two slaves. Their names were Henry Harris and John Harris. The rest of his hands he hired. These consisted of myself, Sandy Jenkins,[3] and Handy Caldwell. Henry and John were quite intelligent, and in a very little while after I went there, I succeeded in creating in them a strong desire to learn how to read. This desire soon sprang up in the others also. They very soon mustered up some old spelling-books, and

Why did Douglass open the Sabbath school?

nothing would do but that I must keep a Sabbath school. I agreed to do so, and accordingly devoted my Sundays to teaching these my loved fellow-slaves how to read. Neither of them knew his letters when I went there. Some of the slaves of the neighboring farms found what was going on, and also availed themselves of this little opportunity to learn to read. It was understood, among all who came, that there must be as little display about it as possible. It was necessary to keep our religious masters at St. Michael's unacquainted

---

[3] **Sandy Jenkins.** [This footnote appeared in Douglass's original *Narrative*.] This is the same man who gave me the roots to prevent my being whipped by Mr. Covey. He was "a clever soul." We used frequently to talk about the fight with Covey, and as often as we did so, he would claim my success as the result of the roots which he gave me. This superstition is very common among the more ignorant slaves. A slave seldom dies but that his death is attributed to trickery.

with the fact, that, instead of spending the Sabbath in wrestling, boxing, and drinking whisky, we were trying to learn how to read the will of God; for they had much rather see us engaged in those degrading sports, than to see us behaving like intellectual, moral, and accountable beings. My blood boils as I think of the bloody manner in which Messrs. Wright Fairbanks and Garrison West, both class-leaders, in connection with many others, rushed in upon us with sticks and stones, and broke up our virtuous little Sabbath school, at St. Michael's—all calling themselves Christians! humble followers of the Lord Jesus Christ! But I am again **digressing**.

I held my Sabbath school at the house of a free colored man, whose name I deem it imprudent to mention; for should it be known, it might embarrass him greatly, though the crime of holding the school was committed ten years ago. I had at one time over forty scholars, and those of the right sort, **ardently** desiring to learn. They were of all ages, though mostly men and women. I look back to those Sundays with an amount of pleasure not to be expressed. They were great days to my soul. The work of instructing my dear fellow-slaves was the sweetest engagement with which I was ever blessed. We loved each other, and to leave them at the close of the Sabbath was a severe cross indeed. When I think that these precious souls are today shut up in the prison-house of slavery, my feelings overcome me, and I am almost ready to ask, "Does a righteous God govern the universe? and for what does he hold the thunders in his right hand, if not to smite the oppressor, and deliver the spoiled out of the hand of the spoiler?" These dear souls came not to Sabbath school because it was popular to do so, nor did I teach them because it was reputable to be thus engaged. Every moment they spent in that school, they

Why did his work with the Sabbath school provide so much pleasure for Douglass?

Vocabulary in Place

digress, v. To turn aside from the main subject of a conversation or argument
The judge ordered the witness to stop **digressing** and answer the question.

ardently, adv. Passionately, enthusiastically
William Lloyd Garrison **ardently** embraced the cause of abolition.

How did Douglass dispel the notion— common among slaveholders—that the enslaved were incapable of a love for learning?

were liable to be taken up, and given thirty-nine lashes. They came because they wished to learn. Their minds had been starved by their cruel masters. They had been shut up in mental darkness. I taught them, because it was the delight of my soul to be doing something that looked like bettering the condition of my race. I kept up my school nearly the whole year I lived with Mr. Freeland; and, beside my Sabbath school, I devoted three evenings in the week, during the winter, to teaching the slaves at home. And I have the happiness to know, that several of those who came to Sabbath school learned how to read; and that one, at least, is now free through my agency.

The year passed off smoothly. It seemed only about half as long as the year which preceded it. I went through it without receiving a single blow. I will give Mr. Freeland the credit of being the best master I ever had, TILL I BECAME MY OWN MASTER. For the ease with which I passed the year, I was, however, somewhat indebted to the society of my fellow-slaves. They were noble souls; they not only possessed loving hearts, but brave ones. We were linked and interlinked with each other. I loved them with a love stronger than any thing I have experienced since. It is sometimes said that we slaves do not love and confide in each other. In answer to this assertion, I can say, I never loved any or confided in any people more than my fellow-slaves, and especially those with whom I lived at Mr. Freeland's. I believe we would have died for each other. We never undertook to do any thing, of any importance, without a mutual consultation. We never moved separately. We were one; and as much so by our tempers and dispositions, as by the mutual hardships to which we were necessarily subjected by our condition as slaves.

What kind of relationship did Douglass form with his students at the Sabbath school?

At the close of the year 1834, Mr. Freeland again hired me of my master, for the year 1835. But, by this time, I began to want to live UPON FREE LAND as well as WITH FREELAND; and I was no longer content, therefore, to live with him or any other slaveholder. I began, with the commencement of the year, to prepare myself for a final struggle, which should decide my fate one way or the other. My tendency was upward. I was fast approaching manhood, and year after year had passed, and I was still a slave. These thoughts roused me—I must do something. I therefore resolved that 1835 should not pass without witnessing an attempt, on my part, to secure my liberty. But I was not willing to cherish this determination alone. My fellow-slaves were dear to me. I was anxious to have them participate with me in this, my life-giving determination. I therefore, though with great prudence, commenced early to ascertain their views and feelings in regard to their condition, and to **imbue** their minds with thoughts of freedom. I bent myself to devising ways and means for our escape, and meanwhile strove, on all fitting occasions, to impress them with the gross fraud and inhumanity of slavery. I went first to Henry, next to John, then to the others. I found, in them all, warm hearts and noble spirits. They were ready to hear, and ready to act when a **feasible** plan should be proposed. This was what I wanted. I talked to them of our want of manhood, if we submitted to our enslavement without at least one noble effort to be free. We met often, and consulted frequently, and told our hopes and fears, recounted the difficulties, real and imagined, which we should be called on to meet. At times we were almost disposed to give up, and try to content ourselves with our wretched lot; at others, we were firm and unbending in our determination to go. Whenever we suggested any plan, there was shrinking—the odds were fearful. Our path was beset with the greatest obstacles; and if we succeeded in gaining the end of it, our right to be free was yet questionable—we were yet liable to be returned to bondage. We could see no spot, this side of the ocean, where we could be free. We knew nothing about Canada. Our knowledge of the north did not extend farther than New York; and to go there, and be forever **harassed** with the frightful liability of being returned to slavery—with the certainty of being

What did Douglass mean when he said that the thought of escaping from slavery was a "life-giving determination"?

Was an escaped slave safe once he reached New York?

Vocabulary in Place

imbue, *v.* To inspire or influence; to permeate or saturate
Beethoven strived to **imbue** his Ninth Symphony with hope and grandeur.

feasible, *adj.* Capable of being accomplished, possible
Is it **feasible** to evacuate two million people in a single day?

harass, *v.* To irritate or torment persistently
Mosquitoes and other insects **harassed** us to no end during our picnic.

Narrative of the Life of Frederick Douglass   *131*

treated tenfold worse than before—the thought was truly a horrible one, and one which it was not easy to overcome. The case sometimes stood thus: At every gate through which we were to pass, we saw a watchman—at every ferry a guard—on every bridge a sentinel—and in every wood a patrol. We were hemmed in upon every side. Here were the difficulties, real or imagined—the good to be sought, and the evil to be shunned. On the one hand, there stood slavery, a stern reality, glaring frightfully upon us,—its robes already crimsoned with the blood of millions, and even now feasting itself greedily upon our own flesh. On the other hand, away back in the dim distance, under the flickering light of the north star, behind some craggy hill or snow-covered mountain, stood a doubtful freedom—half frozen—beckoning us to come and share its hospitality. This in itself was sometimes enough to stagger us; but when we permitted ourselves to survey the road, we were frequently appalled. Upon either side we saw grim death, assuming the most horrid shapes. Now it was starvation, causing us to eat our own flesh;—now we were contending with the waves, and were drowned;—now we were overtaken, and torn to pieces by the fangs of the terrible bloodhound. We were stung by scorpions, chased by wild beasts, bitten by snakes, and finally, after having nearly reached the desired spot,—after swimming rivers, encountering wild beasts, sleeping in the woods, suffering hunger and nakedness,—we were overtaken by our pursuers, and, in our resistance, we were shot dead upon the spot! I say, this picture sometimes appalled us, and made us

> "rather bear those ills we had,
> Than fly to others, that we knew not of."[4]

In coming to a fixed determination to run away, we did more than Patrick Henry, when he resolved upon liberty or death.[5] With

What risks did Douglass and the others take when they attempted to escape? Why were they willing to take such risks?

---

[4] **rather bear . . . that we knew not of.** From Shakespeare's *Hamlet*, Act III, Scene i

[5] **Patrick Henry . . . liberty or death.** Douglass paraphrased American patriot and orator Patrick Henry's (1736–1799) famous speech in which he said, "give me liberty or give me death."

us it was a doubtful liberty at most, and almost certain death if we failed. For my part, I should prefer death to hopeless bondage.

Sandy, one of our number, gave up the notion, but still encouraged us. Our company then consisted of Henry Harris, John Harris, Henry Bailey, Charles Roberts, and myself. Henry Bailey was my uncle, and belonged to my master. Charles married my aunt: he belonged to my master's father-in-law, Mr. William Hamilton.

The plan we finally concluded upon was, to get a large canoe belonging to Mr. Hamilton, and upon the Saturday night previous to Easter holidays, paddle directly up the Chesapeake Bay. On our arrival at the head of the bay, a distance of seventy or eighty miles from where we lived, it was our purpose to turn our canoe adrift, and follow the guidance of the north star till we got beyond the limits of Maryland. Our reason for taking the water route was, that we were less liable to be suspected as runaways; we hoped to be regarded as fishermen; whereas, if we should take the land route, we should be subjected to interruptions of almost every kind. Any one having a white face, and being so disposed, could stop us, and subject us to examination.

The week before our intended start, I wrote several protections, one for each of us. As well as I can remember, they were in the following words, to wit:

How did Douglass use literacy as a tool in his plans to escape?

"This is to certify that I, the undersigned, have given the bearer, my servant, full liberty to go to Baltimore, and spend the Easter holidays. Written with mine own hand, &c., 1835.

"WILLIAM HAMILTON,
"Near St. Michael's, in Talbot county, Maryland."

We were not going to Baltimore; but, in going up the bay, we went toward Baltimore, and these protections were only intended to protect us while on the bay.

As the time drew near for our departure, our anxiety became more and more intense. It was truly a matter of life and death with us. The strength of our determination was about to be fully tested. At this time, I was very active in explaining every difficulty, removing every doubt, dispelling every fear, and inspiring all with

As the leader of the group, what did Douglass do as the time for departure drew near?

the firmness indispensable to success in our undertaking; assuring them that half was gained the instant we made the move; we had talked long enough; we were now ready to move; if not now, we never should be; and if we did not intend to move now, we had as well fold our arms, sit down, and acknowledge ourselves fit only to be slaves. This, none of us were prepared to acknowledge. Every man stood firm; and at our last meeting, we pledged ourselves afresh, in the most solemn manner, that, at the time appointed, we would certainly start in pursuit of freedom. This was in the middle of the week, at the end of which we were to be off. We went, as usual, to our several fields of labor, but with bosoms highly agitated with thoughts of our truly hazardous undertaking. We tried to conceal our feelings as much as possible; and I think we succeeded very well.

After a painful waiting, the Saturday morning, whose night was to witness our departure, came. I hailed it with joy, bring what of sadness it might. Friday night was a sleepless one for me. I probably felt more anxious than the rest, because I was, by common consent, at the head of the whole affair. The responsibility of success or failure lay heavily upon me. The glory of the one, and the confusion of the other, were alike mine. The first two hours of that morning were such as I never experienced before, and hope never to again. Early in the morning, we went, as usual, to the field. We were spreading manure;[6] and all at once, while thus engaged, I was overwhelmed with an indescribable feeling, in the fullness of which I turned to Sandy, who was near by, and said, "We are betrayed!" "Well," said he, "that thought has this moment struck me." We said no more. I was never more certain of any thing.

What did Douglass mean when he said, "we are betrayed"?

The horn was blown as usual, and we went up from the field to the house for breakfast. I went for the form, more than for want of any thing to eat that morning. Just as I got to the house, in looking out at the lane gate, I saw four white men, with two colored men. The white men were on horseback, and the colored ones were walking behind, as if tied. I watched them a few moments till they got up to our lane gate. Here they halted, and tied the colored men

---

[6] **manure.** Waste from livestock used to fertilize crops

to the gate-post. I was not yet certain as to what the matter was. In a few moments, in rode Mr. Hamilton, with a speed betokening[7] great excitement. He came to the door, and inquired if Master William was in. He was told he was at the barn. Mr. Hamilton, without dismounting, rode up to the barn with extraordinary speed. In a few moments, he and Mr. Freeland returned to the house. By this time, the three constables rode up, and in great haste dismounted, tied their horses, and met Master William and Mr. Hamilton returning from the barn; and after talking awhile, they all walked up to the kitchen door. There was no one in the kitchen but myself and John. Henry and Sandy were up at the barn. Mr. Freeland put his head in at the door, and called me by name, saying, there were some gentlemen at the door who wished to see me. I stepped to the door, and inquired what they wanted. They at once seized me, and, without giving me any satisfaction, tied me—lashing my hands closely together. I insisted upon knowing what the matter was. They at length said, that they had learned I had been in a "scrape,"[8] and that I was to be examined before my master; and if their information proved false, I should not be hurt.

In a few moments, they succeeded in tying John. They then turned to Henry, who had by this time returned, and commanded him to cross his hands. "I won't!" said Henry, in a firm tone, indicating his readiness to meet the consequences of his refusal. "Won't you?" said Tom Graham, the constable. "No, I won't!" said Henry, in a still stronger tone. With this, two of the constables pulled out their shining pistols, and swore, by their Creator, that they would make him cross his hands or kill him. Each cocked his pistol, and, with fingers on the trigger, walked up to Henry, saying, at the same time, if he did not cross his hands, they would blow his damned heart out. "Shoot me, shoot me!" said Henry; "you can't kill me but once. Shoot, shoot,—and be damned! I WON'T BE TIED!" This he said in a tone of loud defiance; and at the same time, with a motion as quick as lightning, he with one single stroke dashed the pistols from

In what way did Henry demonstrate his bravery and his determination to maintain his dignity?

---

[7] **betokening.** Giving evidence that something will happen before it actually occurs

[8] **scrape.** A scuffle or fight

the hand of each constable. As he did this, all hands fell upon him, and, after beating him some time, they finally overpowered him, and got him tied.

During the scuffle, I managed, I know not how, to get my pass out, and, without being discovered, put it into the fire. We were all now tied; and just as we were to leave for Easton jail, Betsy Freeland, mother of William Freeland, came to the door with her hands full of biscuits, and divided them between Henry and John. She then delivered herself of a speech, to the following effect:—addressing herself to me, she said, "YOU DEVIL! YOU YELLOW DEVIL! it was you that put it into the heads of Henry and John to run away. But for you, you long-legged mulatto devil! Henry nor John would never have thought of such a thing." I made no reply, and was immediately hurried off towards St. Michael's. Just a moment previous to the scuffle with Henry, Mr. Hamilton suggested the **propriety** of making a search for the protections which he had understood Frederick had written for himself and the rest. But, just at the moment he was about carrying his proposal into effect, his aid was needed in helping to tie Henry; and the excitement attending the scuffle caused them either to forget, or to deem it unsafe, under the circumstances, to search. So we were not yet convicted of the intention to run away.

When we got about half way to St. Michael's, while the constables having us in charge were looking ahead, Henry inquired of me what he should do with his pass. I told him to eat it with his biscuit, and own nothing; and we passed the word around, "OWN NOTHING;" and "OWN NOTHING!" said we all. Our confidence in each other was unshaken. We were resolved to succeed or fail together, after the calamity had befallen us as much as before. We were now prepared for any thing. We were to be dragged that morning fifteen miles behind horses, and then to be placed in the Easton jail. When we reached St. Michael's, we underwent a sort of examination. We all denied that we ever intended to run away. We

Why was Betsy Freeland so angry at Douglass?

Was Douglass lucky that the slave owners and constable did not discover his forged notes? What might have happened if they had known about the notes?

Vocabulary in Place

propriety, *n.* That which is proper or socially acceptable
   Mrs. Bradenton questioned the **propriety** of Harvey's remarks in class.

did this more to bring out the evidence against us, than from any hope of getting clear of being sold; for, as I have said, we were ready for that. The fact was, we cared but little where we went, so we went together. Our greatest concern was about separation. We dreaded that more than any thing this side of death. We found the evidence against us to be the testimony of one person; our master would not tell who it was; but we came to a unanimous decision among ourselves as to who their informant was. We were sent off to the jail at Easton. When we got there, we were delivered up to the sheriff, Mr. Joseph Graham, and by him placed in jail. Henry, John, and myself, were placed in one room together—Charles, and Henry Bailey, in another. Their object in separating us was to hinder **concert.**

We had been in jail scarcely twenty minutes, when a swarm of slave traders, and agents for slave traders, flocked into jail to look at us, and to ascertain if we were for sale. Such a set of beings I never saw before! I felt myself surrounded by so many fiends from perdition.[9] A band of pirates never looked more like their father, the devil. They laughed and grinned over us, saying, "Ah, my boys! we have got you, haven't we?" And after taunting us in various ways, they one by one went into an examination of us, with intent to ascertain our value. They would impudently ask us if we would not like to have them for our masters. We would make them no answer, and leave them to find out as best they could. Then they would curse and swear at us, telling us that they could take the devil out of us in a very little while, if we were only in their hands.

While in jail, we found ourselves in much more comfortable quarters than we expected when we went there. We did not get much to eat, nor that which was very good; but we had a good clean room, from the windows of which we could see what was going on in the street, which was very much better than though we had been placed

Why did they want to "bring out the evidence" against themselves? What were they hoping to learn?

Why did the slave traders appear?

---

[9] **perdition.** Hell, the place of punishment after death

Vocabulary in Place

concert, *n.* Communication of and agreement in actions or beliefs
After two days of negotiation, our ideas were finally in **concert.**

Narrative of the Life of Frederick Douglass   *137*

in one of the dark, damp cells. Upon the whole, we got along very well, so far as the jail and its keeper were concerned. Immediately after the holidays were over, contrary to all our expectations, Mr. Hamilton and Mr. Freeland came up to Easton, and took Charles, the two Henrys, and John, out of jail, and carried them home, leaving me alone. I regarded this separation as a final one. It caused me more pain than any thing else in the whole transaction. I was ready for any thing rather than separation. I supposed that they had consulted together, and had decided that, as I was the whole cause of the intention of the others to run away, it was hard to make the innocent suffer with the guilty; and that they had, therefore, concluded to take the others home, and sell me, as a warning to the others that remained. It is due to the noble Henry to say, he seemed almost as reluctant at leaving the prison as at leaving home to come to the prison. But we knew we should, in all probability, be separated, if we were sold; and since he was in their hands, he concluded to go peaceably home.

Why was Douglass left alone?

138

I was now left to my fate. I was all alone, and within the walls of a stone prison. But a few days before, and I was full of hope. I expected to have been safe in a land of freedom; but now I was covered with gloom, sunk down to the utmost despair. I thought the possibility of freedom was gone. I was kept in this way about one week, at the end of which, Captain Auld, my master, to my surprise and utter astonishment, came up, and took me out, with the intention of sending me, with a gentleman of his acquaintance, into Alabama. But, from some cause or other, he did not send me to Alabama, but concluded to send me back to Baltimore, to live again with his brother Hugh, and to learn a trade.

What did Douglass fear would happen to him? What actually happened?

Thus, after an absence of three years and one month, I was once more permitted to return to my old home at Baltimore. My master sent me away, because there existed against me a very great prejudice in the community, and he feared I might be killed.

In a few weeks after I went to Baltimore, Master Hugh hired me to Mr. William Gardner, an extensive ship-builder, on Fell's Point. I was put there to learn how to calk.[10] It, however, proved a very unfavorable place for the accomplishment of this object. Mr. Gardner was engaged that spring in building two large man-of-war brigs,[11] professedly for the Mexican government. The vessels were to be launched in the July of that year, and in failure thereof, Mr. Gardner was to lose a considerable sum; so that when I entered, all was hurry. There was no time to learn any thing. Every man had to do that which he knew how to do. In entering the shipyard, my orders from Mr. Gardner were, to do whatever the carpenters commanded me to do. This was placing me at the beck and call of about seventy-five men. I was to regard all these as masters. Their word was to be my law. My situation was a most trying one. At times I needed a dozen pair of hands. I was called a dozen ways in the space

What work did Douglass begin to do on going to Baltimore?

10 **calk.** Variant of *caulk.* To make watertight by sealing. Nineteenth-century shipbuilders typically used tarred oakum (fibers from unraveled ropes) to seal the seams between a ship's wooden planks.

11 **man-of-war brigs.** A *man-of-war* was a large warship. *Brig* is short for *brigantine*, a large, two-masted sailing ship.

of a single minute. Three or four voices would strike my ear at the same moment. It was—"Fred., come help me to cant this timber here."—"Fred., come carry this timber yonder."—"Fred., bring that roller here."—"Fred., go get a fresh can of water."—"Fred., come help saw off the end of this timber."—"Fred., go quick, and get the crowbar."—"Fred., hold on the end of this fall."—"Fred., go to the blacksmith's shop, and get a new punch."—"Hurra, Fred.! run and bring me a cold chisel."—"I say, Fred., bear a hand, and get up a fire as quick as lightning under that steam-box."—"Halloo, . . . ! come, turn this grindstone."—"Come, come! move, move! and BOWSE[12] this timber forward."—"I say, darky, blast your eyes, why don't you heat up some pitch?"—"Halloo! halloo! halloo!" (Three voices at the same time.) "Come here!—Go there!—Hold on where you are! Damn you, if you move, I'll knock your brains out!"

This was my school for eight months; and I might have remained there longer, but for a most horrid fight I had with four of the white apprentices, in which my left eye was nearly knocked out, and I was horribly mangled in other respects. The facts in the case were these: Until a very little while after I went there, white and black ship-carpenters worked side by side, and no one seemed to see any impropriety in it. All hands seemed to be very well satisfied. Many of the black carpenters were freemen. Things seemed to be going on very well. All at once, the white carpenters knocked off, and said they would not work with free colored workmen. Their reason for this, as alleged, was, that if free colored carpenters were encouraged, they would soon take the trade into their own hands, and poor white men would be thrown out of employment. They therefore felt called upon at once to put a stop to it. And, taking advantage of Mr. Gardner's necessities, they broke off, swearing they would work no longer, unless he would discharge his black carpenters. Now, though this did not extend to me in form, it did reach me in fact. My fellow-apprentices very soon began to feel it degrading to them to work with me. They began to put on airs, and talk about the " . . ." taking the country, saying we all ought to be killed; and, being encouraged by

How was Douglass treated by white workers of the shipyard?

Why did the white workers make things so hard for Douglass?

Racist epithets in the original text have here been deleted.
—The Editors

---

12 **Bowse.** Variant of *bouse.* A nautical term meaning to hoist or pull.

the journeymen,[13] they commenced making my condition as hard as they could, by hectoring me around, and sometimes striking me. I, of course, kept the vow I made after the fight with Mr. Covey, and struck back again, regardless of consequences; and while I kept them from combining, I succeeded very well; for I could whip the whole of them, taking them separately. They, however, at length combined,

What vow had Douglass made after the fight with Mr. Covey?

and came upon me, armed with sticks, stones, and heavy handspikes. One came in front with a half brick. There was one at each side of me, and one behind me. While I was attending to those in front, and on either side, the one behind ran up with the handspike, and struck me a heavy blow upon the head. It stunned me. I fell, and with this they all ran upon me, and fell to beating me with their fists. I let them lay on for a while, gathering strength.

Photograph entitled "Building the SS Frederick Douglass." This ship, named after Frederick Douglass, was built in 1943 not far from the shipyard in Baltimore where Douglass worked as a caulker in 1835. Library of Congress. LC-USW3-024169-C. Used by Permission

In an instant, I gave a sudden surge, and rose to my hands and knees. Just as I did that, one of their number gave me, with his heavy boot, a powerful kick in the left eye. My eyeball seemed to have burst. When they saw my eye closed, and badly swollen, they left me. With this I seized the handspike, and for a time pursued them. But here the carpenters interfered, and I thought I might as well give it up. It was impossible to stand my hand against so many. All this took place in sight of not less than fifty white ship-carpenters, and not one interposed a friendly word; but some cried, "Kill the damned . . . ! Kill him! kill him! He struck a white person." I found my only

Racist epithets in the original text have here been deleted.
—The Editors

---

13 **journeymen.** Skilled workers or craftsmen who have passed through the apprentice stage

chance for life was in flight. I succeeded in getting away without an additional blow, and barely so; for to strike a white man is death by Lynch law,[14]—and that was the law in Mr. Gardner's ship-yard; nor is there much of any other out of Mr. Gardner's ship-yard.

I went directly home, and told the story of my wrongs to Master Hugh; and I am happy to say of him, irreligious[15] as he was, his conduct was heavenly, compared with that of his brother Thomas under similar circumstances. He listened attentively to my narration of the circumstances leading to the savage outrage, and gave many proofs of his strong **indignation** at it. The heart of my once overkind mistress was again melted into pity. My puffed-out eye and blood-covered face moved her to tears. She took a chair by me, washed the blood from my face, and, with a mother's tenderness, bound up my head, covering the wounded eye with a lean piece of fresh beef. It was almost compensation for my suffering to witness, once more, a manifestation of kindness from this, my once affectionate old mistress. Master Hugh was very much enraged. He gave expression to his feelings by pouring out curses upon the heads of those who did the deed. As soon as I got a little the better of my bruises, he took me with him to Esquire Watson's, on Bond Street, to see what could be done about the matter. Mr. Watson inquired who saw the assault committed. Master Hugh told him it was done in Mr. Gardner's ship-yard at midday, where there were a large company of men at work. "As to that," he said, "the deed was done, and there was no question as to who did it." His answer was, he could do nothing in the case, unless some white man would come forward and testify. He could

How did Master Hugh react when he learned what had happened to Douglass?

---

[14]**Lynch law.** Punishment by hanging—usually by groups of vigilantes, without due process of law—named after Captain William Lynch of Pittsylvania County, Virginia

[15]**irreligious.** Hostile or indifferent to religion

Vocabulary in Place
indignation, *n.* Anger provoked by injustice or wrongdoing
Public **indignation** over the verdict in the Rodney King trial sparked riots in Los Angeles in 1993.

issue no warrant on my word. If I had been killed in the presence of a thousand colored people, their testimony combined would have been insufficient to have arrested one of the murderers. Master Hugh, for once, was compelled to say this state of things was too bad. Of course, it was impossible to get any white man to volunteer his testimony in my behalf, and against the white young men. Even those who may have sympathized with me were not prepared to do this. It required a degree of courage unknown to them to do so; for just at that time, the slightest manifestation of humanity toward a colored person was denounced as abolitionism, and that name subjected its bearer to frightful liabilities. The watchwords of the bloody-minded in that region, and in those days, were, "— the abolitionists!" and "— the . . . !" There was nothing done, and probably nothing would have been done if I had been killed. Such was, and such remains, the state of things in the Christian city of Baltimore.

What legal options were available to Douglass?

Racist epithets and profanity in the original text have here been deleted.
—The Editors

Master Hugh, finding he could get no **redress**, refused to let me go back again to Mr. Gardner. He kept me himself, and his wife dressed my wound till I was again restored to health. He then took me into the ship-yard of which he was foreman, in the employment of Mr. Walter Price. There I was immediately set to calking, and very soon learned the art of using my mallet and irons. In the course of one year from the time I left Mr. Gardner's, I was able to command the highest wages given to the most experienced calkers. I was now of some importance to my master. I was bringing him from six to seven dollars per week. I sometimes brought him nine dollars per week: my wages were a dollar and a half a day. After learning how to calk, I sought my own employment, made my own contracts, and collected the money which I earned. My pathway became much more smooth than before; my condition was now much more comfortable. When I could get no calking to do, I did nothing. During these leisure times,

How did Douglass's life improve after he no longer had to go to Mr. Gardner's shipyard?

Vocabulary in Place

redress, *n.* Compensation for a wrong, loss, or injury
The lawyer promised her clients that they would receive adequate **redress** for their injuries.

---

those old notions about freedom would steal over me again. When in Mr. Gardner's employment, I was kept in such a perpetual whirl of excitement, I could think of nothing, scarcely, but my life; and in thinking of my life, I almost forgot my liberty. I have observed this in my experience of slavery,—that whenever my condition was improved, instead of its increasing my contentment, it only increased my desire to be free, and set me to thinking of plans to gain my freedom. I have found that, to make a contented slave, it is necessary to make a thoughtless one. It is necessary to darken his moral and mental vision, and, as far as possible, to annihilate the power of reason. He must be able to detect no inconsistencies in slavery; he must be made to feel that slavery is right; and he can be brought to that only when he ceases to be a man.

I was now getting, as I have said, one dollar and fifty cents per day. I contracted for it; I earned it; it was paid to me; it was rightfully my own; yet, upon each returning Saturday night, I was compelled to deliver every cent of that money to Master Hugh. And why? Not because he earned it,—not because he had any hand in earning it,—not because I owed it to him,—nor because he possessed the slightest shadow of a right to it; but solely because he had the power to compel me to give it up. The right of the grim-**visaged** pirate upon the high seas is exactly the same. ▨

What happened to Douglass's wages?

In what sense was Master Hugh like a pirate?

Vocabulary in Place

visaged, *adj.* Faced. From the noun *visage,* meaning "face."
 The circus employed a famous sad-**visaged** clown.

A Closer Look

Recalling (just the facts)

1. What did the slaveholders expect the enslaved to do during the holidays? Provide examples from the text.

2. Who was Mr. Freeland? Was he a religious man?

3. What was Douglass determined to do during 1835? Why?

4. To what was Douglass referring when he told his friends to "own nothing"?

5. Why did white workers in the shipyard fear the presence of black workers?

Interpreting (delving deeper)

1. Why did Douglass believe that the holidays were actually representative of the "gross fraud, wrong and inhumanity of slavery"?

2. Compare and contrast Mr. Freeland and Mr. Covey. How were they similar in terms of their position in society? How did they differ as slaveholders?

3. Was Douglass confident that he and the others would succeed in escaping?

4. What was Douglass's worst fear while he was in jail? What actually happened?

5. How were Douglass's experiences working in the shipyard even worse than his experiences as a field hand?

Synthesizing (putting it all together)

Describe three important lessons that Douglass learned during the course of Chapter 10, Part B, regarding the nature of slavery and of slaveholders, the difficulties of escaping from slavery, and the treatment that he was likely to receive from whites if and when he ever actually escaped.

Also, explain why—at the end of the chapter, after his situation had improved somewhat—Douglass's desire to escape had not decreased. ■

Extensions

Writing

Writing Critically about Conflict. At the heart of every good story are one or more **conflicts,** or struggles that the main character faces. An **external conflict** is one that occurs between a character and an outside force, such as another character, a natural occurrence, or a culture as a whole. If a character found himself struggling to stay alive in a hurricane, that would be an example of an external conflict. An **internal conflict** is one that takes place within a character. If a character were struggling between becoming a priest and getting married and having a family, that would be an example of an internal conflict. Conflicts are central to all works of fiction, but nonfiction works like Douglass's *Narrative* are often full of conflicts as well. In nonfiction works, particularly historical and autobiographical works, conflicts are often between competing groups.

Reread the section of this chapter that deals with Douglass's conflict with the other shipyard workers. Who were these people? How did their conditions differ from Douglass's? What did they want? Why did they view Douglass as a threat? How did they react to Douglass as a result? Do you think that people often react to events and to other people out of economic motivations? Think about these questions. Then write a paragraph describing the conflict and its causes.

—Make sure that your paragraph has a topic sentence that states your main idea.

—Use details from the chapter to support your main idea.

—After writing your rough draft, read over your paragraph. Make sure that a reader who is not already familiar with Douglass's *Narrative* will know what you are talking about. Revise your work, if necessary, with such a reader in mind.

—After you have revised your work, make a clean copy, and proofread for errors in grammar, usage, mechanics, and spelling. Refer to the Proofreading Checklist on pages 172-73. ■

Extensions

History and Geography

Fugitive Slave Laws. In 1793, Congress passed the first
of two major Fugitive Slave Laws. The text of this law
read as follows:

*ART. 4. For the better security of the peace and friendship now
entered into by the contracting parties, against all infractions of the
same, by the citizens of either party, to the prejudice of the other, neither party shall proceed
to the infliction of punishments on the citizens of the other, otherwise than by securing
the offender, or offenders, by imprisonment, or any other competent means, till a fair and
impartial trial can be had by judges or juries of both parties, as near as can be, to the laws,
customs, and usages of the contracting parties, and natural justice: the mode of such trials
to be hereafter fixed by the wise men of the United States, in congress assembled, with the
assistance of such deputies of the Delaware nation, as may be appointed to act in concert
with them in adjusting this matter to their mutual liking. And it is further agreed between
the parties aforesaid, that neither shall entertain, or give countenance to, the enemies of the
other, or protect, in their respective states, criminal fugitives, servants, or slaves, but the same
to apprehend and secure, and deliver to the state or states, to which such enemies, criminals,
servants, or slaves, respectively below [sic].*

Discuss with your classmates why, in the light of this law, Douglass says in
Chapter 10 that

> We could see no spot, this side of the ocean, where we could be
> free. We knew nothing about Canada. Our knowledge of the north
> did not extend farther than New York; and to go there, and be forever
> harassed with the frightful liability of being returned to slavery—with the
> certainty of being treated tenfold worse than before—the thought was
> truly a horrible one, and one which it was not easy to overcome. ■

Chapter 11

I now come to that part of my life during which I planned, and finally succeeded in making, my escape from slavery. But before narrating any of the peculiar circumstances, I deem it proper to make known my intention not to state all the facts connected with the transaction. My reasons for pursuing this course may be understood from the following: First, were I to give a minute statement of all the facts, it is not only possible, but quite probable, that others would thereby be involved in the most embarrassing difficulties. Secondly, such a statement would most undoubtedly induce greater vigilance on the part of slaveholders than has existed heretofore among them; which would, of course, be the means of guarding a door whereby some dear brother bondman might escape his galling chains. I deeply regret the necessity that impels me to suppress anything of importance connected with my experience in slavery. It would afford me great pleasure indeed, as well as materially add to the interest of my narrative, were I at liberty to gratify a curiosity, which I know exists in the minds of many, by an accurate statement of all the facts pertaining to my most fortunate escape. But I must deprive myself of this pleasure, and the curious of the gratification which such a statement would afford. I would allow myself to suffer under the greatest **imputations** which evil-minded men might suggest, rather than **exculpate** myself, and thereby run the hazard of closing the

Why might Douglass's "brother bondsmen" have been prevented from escaping if he gave details of his own escape?

Vocabulary in Place

imputation, *n.* The act of attributing fault or responsibility to
  Marieke resented the **imputation** that she had cheated.

exculpate, *v.* To clear of guilt or blame
  The faculty review committee **exculpated** Marieke once and for all.

148

slightest avenue by which a brother slave might clear himself of the chains and fetters[1] of slavery.

I have never approved of the very public manner in which some of our western friends have conducted what they call the UNDERGROUND RAILROAD, but which I think, by their open declarations, has been made most emphatically the UPPERGROUND RAILROAD. I honor those good men and women for their noble daring, and applaud them for willingly subjecting themselves to bloody persecution, by openly avowing their participation in the escape of slaves. I, however, can see very little good resulting from such a course, either to themselves or the slaves escaping; while, upon the other hand, I see and feel assured that those open declarations are a positive evil to the slaves remaining, who are seeking to escape. They do nothing towards enlightening the slave, whilst they do much towards enlightening the master. They stimulate him to greater watchfulness, and enhance his power to capture his slave. We owe something to the slave south of the line as well as to those north of it; and in aiding the latter on their way to freedom, we should be careful to do nothing which would be likely to hinder the former from escaping from slavery. I would keep the merciless slaveholder profoundly ignorant of the means of flight adopted by the slave. I would leave him to imagine himself surrounded by myriads of invisible tormentors, ever ready to snatch from his infernal grasp his trembling prey. Let him be left to feel his way in the dark; let darkness **commensurate** with his crime hover over him; and let him feel that at every step he takes, in pursuit of the flying bondman, he is running the frightful risk of having his hot brains dashed out by an invisible agency. Let us render the tyrant no aid; let us not hold the

What did Douglass mean when he called it the "Upperground" Railroad?

Why did Douglass not approve of the fact that some "conductors" of the Underground Railroad openly publicized their efforts?

---

[1] **fetters.** Chains or shackles, especially for the hands and feet

---

Vocabulary in Place

commensurate, *adj.* Corresponding in size or degree
  Mike thought he deserved a salary **commensurate** with his advanced skills and experience.

---

light by which he can trace the footprints of our flying brother. But enough of this. I will now proceed to the statement of those facts, connected with my escape, for which I am alone responsible, and for which no one can be made to suffer but myself.

In the early part of the year 1838, I became quite restless. I could see no reason why I should, at the end of each week, pour the reward of my toil into the purse of my master. When I carried to him my weekly wages, he would, after counting the money, look me in the face with a robber-like fierceness, and ask, "Is this all?" He was satisfied with nothing less than the last cent. He would, however, when I made him six dollars, sometimes give me six cents, to encourage me. It had the opposite effect. I regarded it as a sort of admission of my right to the whole. The fact that he gave me any part of my wages was proof, to my mind, that he believed me entitled to the whole of them. I always felt worse for having received anything; for I feared that the giving me a few cents would ease his conscience, and make him feel himself to be a pretty honorable sort of robber. My discontent grew upon me. I was ever on the look-out for means of escape; and, finding no direct means, I determined to try to hire my time, with a view of getting money with which to make my escape. In the spring of 1838, when Master Thomas came to Baltimore to purchase his spring goods, I got an opportunity, and applied to him to allow me to hire my time. He unhesitatingly refused my request, and told me this was another stratagem by which to escape. He told me I could go nowhere but that he could get me; and that, in the event of my running away, he should spare no pains in his efforts to catch me. He **exhorted** me to content myself, and be obedient. He told me, if I would be happy, I must lay out no plans for the future. He said, if I behaved myself properly, he would take care of me. Indeed, he advised me to complete thoughtlessness of the future, and taught me to depend solely upon him for happiness.

Why did Douglass feel worse when his "master" gave him back part of his wages?

Vocabulary in Place
exhort, *v.* To urge by strong argument, advise The coach **exhorted** the players to get to bed early before tomorrow's big game.

He seemed to see fully the pressing necessity of setting aside my intellectual nature, in order to [encourage my] contentment in slavery. But in spite of him, and even in spite of myself, I continued to think, and to think about the injustice of my enslavement, and the means of escape.

About two months after this, I applied to Master Hugh for the privilege of hiring my time. He was not acquainted with the fact that I had applied to Master Thomas, and had been refused. He too, at first, seemed disposed to refuse; but, after some reflection, he granted me the privilege, and proposed the following terms: I was to be allowed all my time, make all contracts with those for whom I worked, and find my own employment; and, in return for this liberty, I was to pay him three dollars at the end of each week; find myself in calking tools, and in board and clothing. My board was two dollars and a half per week. This, with the wear and tear of clothing and calking tools, made my regular expenses about six dollars per week. This amount I was compelled to make up, or relinquish the privilege of hiring my time. Rain or shine, work or no work, at the end of each week the money must be forthcoming, or I must give up my privilege. This arrangement, it will be perceived, was decidedly in my master's favor. It relieved him of all need of looking after me. His money was sure. He received all the benefits of slaveholding without its evils; while I endured all the evils of a slave, and suffered all the care and anxiety of a freeman. I found it a hard bargain. But, hard as it was, I thought it better than the old mode of getting along. It was a step towards freedom to be allowed to bear the responsibilities of a freeman, and I was determined to hold on upon it. I bent myself to the work of making money. I was ready to work at night as well as day, and by the most untiring **perseverance** and industry, I made enough to meet my expenses, and lay up a little money every week. I went on thus from May till August. Master Hugh then refused to

Why did Douglass go to Master Hugh?

In what sense did Douglass suffer the "care and anxiety of a free man"?

Vocabulary in Place

perseverance, *n.* Steady persistence, determination
Marathon runners are models of **perseverance.**

---

allow me to hire my time longer. The ground for his refusal was a failure on my part, one Saturday night, to pay him for my week's time. This failure was occasioned by my attending a camp meeting about ten miles from Baltimore. During the week, I had entered into an engagement with a number of young friends to start from Baltimore to the camp ground early Saturday evening; and being detained by my employer, I was unable to get down to Master Hugh's without disappointing the company. I knew that Master Hugh was in no special need of the money that night. I therefore decided to go to camp meeting, and upon my return pay him the three dollars. I staid at the camp meeting one day longer than I intended when I left. But as soon as I returned, I called upon him to pay him what he considered his due. I found him very angry; he could scarce restrain his **wrath**. He said he had a great mind to give me a severe whipping. He wished to know how I dared go out of the city without asking his permission. I told him I hired my time and while I paid him the price which he asked for it, I did not know that I was bound to ask him when and where I should go. This reply troubled him; and, after reflecting a few moments, he turned to me, and said I should hire my time no longer; that the next thing he should know of, I would be running away. Upon the same plea, he told me to bring my tools and clothing home forthwith. I did so; but instead of seeking work, as I had been accustomed to do previously to hiring my time, I spent the whole week without the performance of a single stroke of work. I did this in retaliation. Saturday night, he called upon me as usual for my week's wages. I told him I had no wages; I had done no work that week. Here we were upon the point of coming to blows. He raved, and swore his determination to get hold of me. I did not allow myself a single word; but was resolved, if he laid the weight of his hand upon me, it should be blow for blow. He did not strike me, but told me that he would find me in constant employment in future.

Why was Hugh so angry? Why did Douglass's excuse trouble him?

Why did Douglass not work that week?

Vocabulary in Place

wrath, *n.* Extreme anger
  Words cannot describe Mr. Peters's **wrath** after we accidentally shattered his window with the baseball.

I thought the matter over during the next day, Sunday, and finally resolved upon the third day of September, as the day upon which I would make a second attempt to secure my freedom. I now had three weeks during which to prepare for my journey. Early on Monday morning, before Master Hugh had time to make any engagement for me, I went out and got employment of Mr. Butler, at his ship-yard near the drawbridge, upon what is called the City Block, thus making it unnecessary for him to seek employment for me. At the end of the week, I brought him between eight and nine dollars. He seemed very well pleased, and asked why I did not do the same the week before. He little knew what my plans were. My object in working steadily was to remove any suspicion he might entertain of my intent to run away; and in this I succeeded admirably. I suppose he thought I was never better satisfied with my condition than at the very time during which I was planning my escape. The second week passed, and again I carried him my full wages; and so well pleased was he, that he gave me twenty-five cents (quite a large sum for a slaveholder to give a slave) and bade me to make a good use of it. I told him I would.

Did Master Hugh understand Douglass's real meaning when he said that he would make good use of the twenty-five cents?

Things went on without very smoothly indeed, but within there was trouble. It is impossible for me to describe my feelings as the time of my contemplated start drew near. I had a number of warm-hearted friends in Baltimore,—friends that I loved almost as I did my life,—and the thought of being separated from them forever was painful beyond expression. It is my opinion that thousands would escape from slavery, who now remain, but for the strong cords of affection that bind them to their friends. The thought of leaving my friends was decidedly the most painful thought with which I had to contend. The love of them was my tender point, and shook my decision more than all things else. Besides the pain of separation, the dread and apprehension of a failure exceeded what I had experienced at my first attempt. The appalling defeat I then sustained returned to torment me. I felt assured that, if I failed in this attempt, my case would be a hopeless one—it would seal my fate as a slave forever. I could not hope to get off with any thing less than the severest punishment, and being placed beyond the means of escape. It required no very vivid imagination to depict the most frightful scenes through which

What, according to Douglass, kept many enslaved people from trying to escape?

I should have to pass, in case I failed. The wretchedness of slavery, and the blessedness of freedom, were perpetually before me. It was life and death with me. But I remained firm, and, according to my resolution, on the third day of September, 1838, I left my chains, and succeeded in reaching New York without the slightest interruption of any kind. How I did so,—what means I adopted,—what direction I travelled, and by what mode of conveyance,—I must leave unexplained, for the reasons before mentioned.

Why did Douglass choose not to reveal the details of his escape?

I have been frequently asked how I felt when I found myself in a free State. I have never been able to answer the question with any satisfaction to myself. It was a moment of the highest excitement I ever experienced. I suppose I felt as one may imagine the unarmed

Illustration entitled "Twenty-Eight Fugitive Slaves Escaping from the Eastern Shore of Maryland" from the *Underground Railroad,* ca.1860. Special Collections, University of Virginia. Used by Permission.

mariner to feel when he is rescued by a friendly man-of-war from the pursuit of a pirate. In writing to a dear friend, immediately after my arrival at New York, I said I felt like one who had escaped a den of hungry lions. This state of mind, however, very soon subsided; and I was again seized with a feeling of great insecurity and loneliness. I was yet liable to be taken back, and subjected to all the tortures of slavery. This in itself was enough to damp the ardor of my enthusiasm. But the loneliness overcame me. There I was in the midst of thousands, and yet a perfect stranger; without home and without friends, in the midst of thousands of my own brethren—

Why was Douglass so lonely?

children of a common Father, and yet I dared not to unfold to any one of them my sad condition. I was afraid to speak to any one for fear of speaking to the wrong one, and thereby falling into the hands of money-loving kidnappers, whose business it was to lie in wait for the panting fugitive, as the ferocious beasts of the forest lie in wait for their prey. The motto which I adopted when I started from slavery was this—"Trust no man!" I saw in every white man an enemy, and in almost every colored man cause for distrust. It was a most painful situation; and, to understand it, one must needs experience it, or imagine himself in similar circumstances. Let him be a fugitive slave in a strange land—a land given up to be the hunting-ground for slaveholders—whose inhabitants are legalized kidnappers—where he is every moment subjected to the terrible liability of being seized upon by his fellowmen, as the hideous crocodile seizes upon his prey!—I say, let him place himself in my situation—without home or friends—without money or credit—wanting shelter, and no one to give it—wanting bread, and no money to buy it,—and at the same time let him feel that he is pursued by merciless men-hunters, and in total darkness as to what to do, where to go, or where to stay,—perfectly helpless both as to the means of defense and means of escape,—in the midst of plenty, yet suffering the terrible gnawings of hunger,—in the midst of houses, yet having no home,—among fellow-men, yet feeling as if in the midst of wild beasts, whose greediness to swallow up the trembling and half-famished fugitive is only equalled by that with which the monsters of the deep swallow up the helpless fish upon which they subsist,—I say, let him be placed in this most trying situation,—the situation in which I was placed,—then, and not till then, will he fully appreciate the hardships of, and know how to sympathize with, the toil-worn and whip-scarred fugitive slave.

Thank Heaven, I remained but a short time in this distressed situation. I was relieved from it by the humane hand of Mr. DAVID RUGGLES, whose vigilance, kindness, and perseverance, I shall never forget. I am glad of an opportunity to express, as far as words can, the love and gratitude I bear him. Mr. Ruggles is now afflicted with blindness, and is himself in need of the same kind offices which he was once so forward in the performance of toward others. I had

Did Douglass's initial experiences in New York correspond to his expectations of freedom?

In what ways were those who hunted escaped slaves similar to "monsters of the deep"?

been in New York but a few days, when Mr. Ruggles sought me out, and very kindly took me to his boarding-house at the corner of Church and Lespenard Streets. Mr. Ruggles was then very deeply engaged in the memorable DARG case, as well as attending to a number of other fugitive slaves, devising ways and means for their successful escape; and, though watched and hemmed in on almost every side, he seemed to be more than a match for his enemies.

Very soon after I went to Mr. Ruggles, he wished to know of me where I wanted to go; as he deemed it unsafe for me to remain in New York. I told him I was a calker, and should like to go where I could get work. I thought of going to Canada; but he decided against it, and in favor of my going to New Bedford, thinking I should be able to get work there at my trade. At this time, Anna,[2] my intended wife, came on; for I wrote to her immediately after my arrival at New York, (notwithstanding my homeless, houseless, and helpless condition,) informing her of my successful flight, and wishing her to come on forthwith. In a few days after her arrival, Mr. Ruggles called in the Rev. J. W. C. Pennington, who, in the presence of Mr. Ruggles, Mrs. Michaels, and two or three others, performed the marriage ceremony, and gave us a certificate, of which the following is an exact copy:

"This may certify, that I joined together in holy matrimony Frederick Johnson[3] and Anna Murray, as man and wife, in the presence of Mr. David Ruggles and Mrs. Michaels.

"JAMES W. C. PENNINGTON
"NEW YORK, SEPT. 15, 1838"

Upon receiving this certificate, and a five-dollar bill from Mr. Ruggles, I shouldered one part of our baggage, and Anna took up the other, and we set out forthwith to take passage on board of the steamboat John W. Richmond for Newport, on our way to New

Why was New York unsafe?

---

[2] **Anna.** [This footnote appeared in Douglass's original *Narrative*.] She was free.

[3] **Frederick Johnson.** [This footnote appeared in Douglass's original *Narrative*.] I had changed my name from Frederick BAILEY to that of JOHNSON.

Bedford. Mr. Ruggles gave me a letter to a Mr. Shaw in Newport, and told me, in case my money did not serve me to New Bedford, to stop in Newport and obtain further assistance; but upon our arrival at Newport, we were so anxious to get to a place of safety, that, notwithstanding we lacked the necessary money to pay our fare, we decided to take seats in the stage, and promise to pay when we got to New Bedford. We were encouraged to do this by two excellent gentlemen, residents of New Bedford, whose names I afterward ascertained to be Joseph Ricketson and William C. Taber. They seemed at once to understand our circumstances, and gave us such assurance of their friendliness as put us fully at ease in their presence. It was good indeed to meet with such friends, at such a time. Upon reaching New Bedford, we were directed to the house of Mr. Nathan Johnson, by whom we were kindly received, and hospitably provided for. Both Mr. and Mrs. Johnson took a deep and lively interest in our welfare. They proved themselves quite worthy of the name of abolitionists. When the stage-driver found us unable to pay our fare, he held on upon our baggage as security for the debt. I had but to mention the fact to Mr. Johnson, and he forthwith advanced the money.

Why were so many strangers willing to help Douglass?

We now began to feel a degree of safety, and to prepare ourselves for the duties and responsibilities of a life of freedom. On the morning after our arrival at New Bedford, while at the breakfast-table, the question arose as to what name I should be called by. The name given me by my mother was, "Frederick Augustus Washington Bailey." I, however, had dispensed with the two middle names long before I left Maryland so that I was generally known by the name of "Frederick Bailey." I started from Baltimore bearing the name of "Stanley." When I got to New York, I again changed my name to "Frederick Johnson," and thought that would be the last change. But when I got to New Bedford, I found it necessary again to change my name. The reason of this necessity was, that there were so many Johnsons in New Bedford, it was already quite difficult to distinguish between them. I gave Mr. Johnson the privilege of choosing me a name, but told him he must not take from me the name of "Frederick." I must hold on to that, to preserve a sense of my identity. Mr. Johnson had just been reading the "Lady of the Lake,"[4] and at once suggested that

Why was it important to Douglass that he keep his first name?

Why was New Bedford such a strange place to Douglass?

my name be "Douglass." From that time until now I have been called "Frederick Douglass;" and as I am more widely known by that name than by either of the others, I shall continue to use it as my own.

I was quite disappointed at the general appearance of things in New Bedford. The impression which I had received respecting the character and condition of the people of the north, I found to be singularly **erroneous**. I had very strangely supposed, while in slavery, that few of the comforts, and scarcely any of the luxuries, of life were enjoyed at the north, compared with what were enjoyed by the slaveholders of the south. I probably came to this conclusion from the fact that northern people owned no slaves. I supposed that they were about upon a level with the non-slaveholding population of the south. I knew THEY were exceedingly poor, and I had been accustomed to regard their poverty as the necessary consequence of their being non-slaveholders. I had somehow imbibed the opinion that, in the absence of slaves, there could be no wealth, and very little refinement. And upon coming to the north, I expected to meet with a rough, hard-handed, and uncultivated population, living in the most Spartan-like simplicity,[5] knowing nothing of the ease, luxury, pomp, and grandeur of southern slaveholders. Such being my conjectures, any one acquainted with the appearance of New Bedford may very readily infer how palpably I must have seen my mistake.

In the afternoon of the day when I reached New Bedford, I visited the wharves, to take a view of the shipping. Here I found myself surrounded with the strongest proofs of wealth. Lying at the

---

[4] **Lady of the Lake.** A poem by Sir Walter Scott (1771–1832) in which there is a character named Douglas

[5] **Spartan-like simplicity.** Sparta was an ancient Greek city whose citizens were famous for their discipline, military prowess, and distaste for luxurious living. *Spartan* is commonly used as an adjective meaning "self-restrained" and "basic."

Vocabulary in Place
erroneous, *adj.* False, mistaken The view that the heavens were unchanging was proved **erroneous** in 1572 when the astronomer Tycho Brahe observed a supernova, or exploding star.

158

wharves, and riding in the stream, I saw many ships of the finest model, in the best order, and of the largest size. Upon the right and left, I was walled in by granite warehouses of the widest dimensions, stowed to their utmost capacity with the necessaries and comforts of life. Added to this, almost every body seemed to be at work, but noiselessly so, compared with what I had been accustomed to in Baltimore. There were no loud songs heard from those engaged in loading and unloading ships. I heard no deep oaths or horrid curses on the laborer. I saw no whipping of men; but all seemed to go smoothly on. Every man appeared to understand his work, and went at it with a sober, yet cheerful earnestness, which betokened the deep interest which he felt in what he was doing, as well as a sense of his own dignity as a man. To me this looked exceedingly strange. From the wharves I strolled around and over the town, gazing with wonder and admiration at the splendid churches, beautiful dwellings, and finely-cultivated gardens; evincing an amount of wealth, comfort, taste, and refinement, such as I had never seen in any part of slaveholding Maryland.

Every thing looked clean, new, and beautiful. I saw few or no **dilapidated** houses, with poverty-stricken inmates; no half-naked children and barefooted women, such as I had been accustomed to see in Hillsborough, Easton, St. Michael's, and Baltimore. The people looked more able, stronger, healthier, and happier, than those of Maryland. I was for once made glad by a view of extreme wealth, without being saddened by seeing extreme poverty. But the most astonishing as well as the most interesting thing to me was the condition of the colored people, a great many of whom, like myself, had escaped thither as a refuge from the hunters of men. I found many, who had not been seven years out of their chains, living in finer houses, and evidently enjoying more of the comforts of life, than the average of slaveholders in Maryland. I will venture to

What were the living conditions like for the "colored people" of New Bedford?

Vocabulary in Place

dilapidated, *adj.* Broken down, shabby, having fallen into a state of disrepair
It is about time the city did something about all the abandoned, **dilapidated** houses on that street.

---

assert, that my friend Mr. Nathan Johnson (of whom I can say with a grateful heart, "I was hungry, and he gave me meat; I was thirsty, and he gave me drink; I was a stranger, and he took me in")[6] lived in a neater house; dined at a better table; took, paid for, and read, more newspapers; better understood the moral, religious, and political character of the nation,—than nine tenths of the slaveholders in Talbot county Maryland. Yet Mr. Johnson was a working man. His hands were hardened by toil, and not his alone, but those also of Mrs. Johnson. I found the colored people much more spirited than I had supposed they would be. I found among them a determination to protect each other from the blood-thirsty kidnapper, at all hazards. Soon after my arrival, I was told of a circumstance which illustrated their spirit. A colored man and a fugitive slave were on unfriendly terms. The former was heard to threaten the latter with informing his master of his whereabouts. Straightway a meeting was called among the colored people, under the stereotyped notice, "Business of importance!" The betrayer was invited to attend. The people came at the appointed hour, and organized the meeting by appointing a very religious old gentleman as president, who, I believe, made a prayer, after which he addressed the meeting as follows: "FRIENDS, WE HAVE GOT HIM HERE, AND I WOULD RECOMMEND THAT YOU YOUNG MEN JUST TAKE HIM OUTSIDE THE DOOR, AND KILL HIM!" With this, a number of them bolted at him; but they were intercepted by some more timid than themselves, and the betrayer escaped their vengeance, and has not been seen in New Bedford since. I believe there have been no more such threats, and should there be hereafter, I doubt not that death would be the consequence.

I found employment, the third day after my arrival, in stowing a sloop with a load of oil. It was new, dirty, and hard work for me; but I went at it with a glad heart and a willing hand. I was now my own master. It was a happy moment, the rapture of which can be understood only by those who have been slaves. It was the first work, the reward of which was to be entirely my own. There was no Master

To whom did Douglass refer when he mentioned "the blood-thirsty kidnapper"?

What had the "betrayer" done to offend the community?

---

[6]**I was hungry . . . took me in.** Matthew 25:35

Hugh standing ready, the moment I earned the money, to rob me of it. I worked that day with a pleasure I had never before experienced. I was at work for myself and newly-married wife. It was to me the starting-point of a new existence. When I got through with that job, I went in pursuit of a job of calking; but such was the strength of prejudice against color, among the white calkers, that they refused to work with me, and of course I could get no employment.[7] Finding my trade of no immediate benefit, I threw off my calking habiliments, and prepared myself to do any kind of work I could get to do. Mr. Johnson kindly let me have his wood-horse and saw, and I very soon found myself a plenty of work. There was no work too hard—none too dirty. I was ready to saw wood, shovel coal, carry wood, sweep the chimney, or roll oil casks,—all of which I did for nearly three years in New Bedford, before I became known to the anti-slavery world.

In about four months after I went to New Bedford, there came a young man to me, and inquired if I did not wish to take the "Liberator."[8] I told him I did; but, just having made my escape from slavery, I remarked that I was unable to pay for it then. I, however, finally became a subscriber to it. The paper came, and I read it from week to week with such feelings as it would be quite idle for me to attempt to describe. The paper became my meat and my drink. My soul was set all on fire. Its sympathy for my brethren in bonds—its **scathing** denunciations of slaveholders—its faithful exposures of slavery—and its powerful attacks upon the upholders of the institution—sent a thrill of joy through my soul, such as I had never felt before!

What did Douglass mean when he called the Liberator his "meat" and "drink"?

---

[7] **When I got . . . no employment.** [This footnote appeared in Douglass's original *Narrative*.] I am told that colored persons can now get employment at calking in New Bedford—a result of the anti-slavery effort.

[8] **Liberator.** This was William Lloyd Garrison's abolitionist newspaper.

> **Vocabulary in Place**
>
> **scathing,** *adj.* Harshly critical
> Frederick Douglass's **scathing** indictment of slavery inspired many people to join the abolitionist cause.

I had not long been a reader of the "Liberator," before I got a pretty correct idea of the principles, measures and spirit of the anti-slavery reform. I took right hold of the cause. I could do but little; but what I could, I did with a joyful heart, and never felt happier than when in an anti-slavery meeting. I seldom had much to say at the meetings, because what I wanted to say was said so much better by others. But, while attending an anti-slavery convention at Nantucket, on the 11th of August, 1841, I felt strongly moved to speak, and was at the same time much urged to do so by Mr. William C. Coffin, a gentleman who had heard me speak in the colored people's meeting at New Bedford. It was a severe cross, and I took it up reluctantly. The truth was, I felt myself a slave, and the idea of speaking to white people weighed me down. I spoke but a few moments, when I felt a degree of freedom, and said what I desired with considerable ease. From that time until now, I have been engaged in pleading the cause of my brethren—with what success, and with what devotion, I leave those acquainted with my labors to decide. ▓

Why did Douglass feel uneasy, at first, about speaking publicly?

Frederick Douglass went on to become, of course, one of the greatest orators in the history of the United States and one of the leading figures in the movement to abolish slavery. He published a newspaper, *The North Star*. He became a personal friend to President Abraham Lincoln. He worked as the editor and then the publisher of another paper, the *New National Era*, served as a bank president and as a U. S. marshal, lectured widely, and campaigned tirelessly for voting rights for blacks and for women. Near the end of his life, he served as U.S. Consul General to the country of Haiti. These were altogether astonishing accomplishments for a man born into slavery who had to teach himself how to read and write. Those of us who are born into more privileged circumstances have much to learn from this exceptional man and his unconquerable spirit.

—The Editors

A Closer Look

Recalling (just the facts)

1. Why did Douglass object to people talking about their activities on behalf of the Underground Railroad?
2. What reason did Douglass give—even greater than his fear of being caught—for not wanting to embark on his escape?
3. Where did Douglass go when he left Baltimore, and what did he experience on first arriving there? Give examples from the text to support your answer.
4. List three ways in which New Bedford was noticeably different from Talbot County, Maryland, and other places where Douglass lived as a slave.

Interpreting (delving deeper)

1. Did Master Hugh suspect that Douglass was planning to escape? How did Douglass distract Hugh from his real intentions?
2. Did Douglass enjoy life in the town of New Bedford? Why?
3. How did the free black community in New Bedford protect itself from those who would betray the whereabouts of fugitive slaves?
4. What made the *Liberator* such an important newspaper?

Synthesizing (putting it all together)

What message was Douglass sending to slaveholders when he described the wealth, sophistication, and strong work ethic of the inhabitants of New Bedford?

Extension

Writing

Epistolary Form. In literature, a piece of fiction is said to be written in **epistolary form** when it consists of personal letters written by a character (or of a correspondence between two or more characters).

Try your hand at epistolary fiction by writing a letter from the perspective of a recently escaped slave. Answer the following questions on a separate sheet of paper in order to "get to know" your character. Doing this will help you to organize your letter, but you do not have to include all this information in your writing.

—Is your main character a man or woman? How old?
—From where did she escape, and what was it like there?
—Was she alone, or did she escape with a group?
—How long was she on the run?
—Did the escape go according to plan?
—Did she receive assistance from the Underground Railroad?
—Has her experience with freedom, thus far, met her expectations?

Once you have answered these questions, you must decide to whom your letter will be addressed. Your character might be writing to another escaped slave, to someone from the Underground Railroad, to the editor of a newspaper, or even to a former "master"!

Be sure to use plenty of details in your letter, and try to capture your narrator's voice and personality in your writing. Refer to the Resources for Writers on pages 170-73 to refine and polish your rough draft. As an additional exercise, you can trade letters with another student and reply to his or her letter.

Extensions

Theme. The **theme** of a story—whether it is fiction or nonfiction—is the main idea or message that the author is trying to convey. The theme may be some message or comment about society, human nature, or life in general.

A story, especially an autobiographical work like Douglass's *Narrative,* can have more than one theme. Douglass clearly had more than one message to share with his audience.

The following is a list of nine recurring themes in the *Narrative.* Each item on the list describes a theme touched upon repeatedly over the course of the book:

1. The treatment of human beings as **chattel** (property)
2. The importance of **education and literacy**
3. **Hunger** as a driving force behind human action
4. **Freedom** as a basic human need
5. **Separation** of families as an intentional tactic on the part of slaveholders to maintain order
6. The **corrupting** nature of power (i.e., slavery's corruption of the slaveholder)
7. The difference between **professed** religion and actual behavior or practices
8. The **bonds** that develop between oppressed people
9. The need to maintain personal **dignity**

—**Find one example in the book that illustrates each of the themes listed above.** On a separate sheet of paper, write the chapter in which the scene takes place and one sentence briefly summarizing the scene or passage.

—Try to come up with at least one additional theme (major or minor) from the *Narrative* that is not listed above and provide one example from the text to support your idea.

Extensions

—**Select one theme from the list,** and locate at least one additional passage from the text that conveys this theme.

—**Write a one-page essay in which you answer the following questions:** Why did Douglass choose to weave this theme into his *Narrative?* How did Douglass convey this theme to his readers (use the examples that you have located in the text to support your answer)? What can you—as a person living in the twenty-first century—learn from Douglass's treatment of this theme?

—Use the Resources for Writers on pages 170–73 to revise and finalize your draft. ■

A Final Look

Creative Writing

1. Put yourself in their shoes. Write a one-page **journal entry** or **personal letter** from the perspective of one of these characters: *Gore, Severe, Hopkins,* or *Covey; Mr.* or *Mrs. Auld; Sandy Jenkins;* Douglass's *mother* or *grandmother;* or *David Ruggles.*

2. Escape! Write a **short story** about a fugitive slave who is trying to escape to the northern states. Use parts of Douglass's *Narrative* (especially Chapters 10 and 11) as a source of specific details to make your story come alive. You can write your story from the **first-person point of view** (using pronouns like *I* and *we)* or from the **third-person point of view** (using pronouns like *he, she,* and *they).*

3. Your Autobiography. Review the Writing Extension at the end of Chapter 1. For this exercise you will rewrite the autobiographical sketch that you wrote about for that exercise or write a new piece following the same basic guidelines. This time around, however, you will include literary devices that Douglass used throughout his *Narrative.* Your "new" autobiographical sketch should contain at least one example of *each* of the following techniques or tools from your writing toolbox:

—Chiasmus
—Figurative language, including metaphor, simile, and metonymy (one of each)
—Alliteration
—Maxim
—Sensory Imagery ■

A Final Look

Critical Writing

1. Turning Points. Select one of the following scenes from the *Narrative* and write an essay explaining why it was so important in Douglass's life:

- Mr. Auld ordering Mrs. Auld to stop teaching young Douglass his ABCs (Chapter 6)
- The "valuation" after Captain Anthony's death (Chapter 8)
- Douglass's beating Covey and Hughes in a fight (Chapter 10a)

Your essay should address each of the following questions:

- What was Douglass's experience?
- What did Douglass gain or learn from the experience?
- How did the event encourage or inspire him to escape from slavery?
- In what way might this event have helped Douglass to accomplish all the things he did in his lifetime? (Review the biography on pages ix–xviii if necessary).

2. Interpreting One of the Sorrow Songs. Read the story of the captivity of the Israelites in Egypt and their eventual deliverance from bondage. Most enslaved African-Americans would have known the story from the version told in the book of Exodus in the Bible, although this story is also found in the Torah and in the Qur'an. After doing this background reading, look up on the Internet the lyrics to "Go Down, Moses." Then write a piece that explains the sources and significance of the spiritual. ■

Resources for Writers

Audience and Purpose

☐ Is the piece appropriate to the intended audience?

☐ Does the piece have the appropriate level of formality or informality?

☐ Have you included the background information necessary for your audience to follow what you are saying?

☐ Does the piece accomplish the purpose for which it was written?

Style and Voice

☐ Does the piece contain vivid verbs and concrete, precise nouns?

☐ Are your word choices appropriate throughout? Can they be improved upon?

☐ Have you varied the types and lengths of sentences used in the piece?

☐ Will the piece be interesting to your reader?

Structure and Organization

☐ Does the introduction capture the attention of the reader?

☐ Where appropriate, do your paragraphs have topic sentences? Note: An introductory paragraph in a piece of expository writing may lack a topic sentence. Paragraphs in pieces of fictional writing typically do not have topic sentences. Body paragraphs in a piece of expository

Resources for Writers

Revision Checklist (cont.)

writing should have a topic sentence or, at the very least, a main idea.

- [ ] Do the body sentences in those paragraphs with topic sentences support the topic sentences?
- [ ] Do ideas follow one another logically throughout the piece?
- [ ] Have you used transitions to tie your ideas together?

Focus and Elaboration

- [ ] Are your main ideas supported with evidence, specific details, or examples?
- [ ] Have you included any material that is unnecessary or irrelevant to your topic or to the ideas and/or emotions that you are trying to convey?

Questions to Ask about an Essay

- [ ] Does the essay have a clear introduction, body, and conclusion?
- [ ] Does the introduction present a thesis statement, or main idea of the essay as a whole?
- [ ] Does each body paragraph present a main idea, in a topic sentence, that supports the thesis statement?
- [ ] Does the conclusion provide a satisfying ending for the essay? Does it restate or summarize the argument of the essay, make the main point again in another way, call upon the reader to take some action, or otherwise provide a sense of an ending? ▪

Resources for Writers

Manuscript Form

- ☐ Is each paragraph indented?
- ☐ Have you left standard margins (usually one inch) on all sides?
- ☐ If the piece is handwritten, is the writing legible?
- ☐ Does your piece have a title? Is the title written correctly, using uppercase and lowercase letters?
- ☐ Does your name and other information required by your teacher appear on the page in the appropriate place (generally in the upper, right-hand portion of the paper)?

Grammar and Usage

- ☐ Does each verb agree with its subject?
- ☐ Does each pronoun have a clear antecedent and agree with it?
- ☐ Are commonly confused pronouns such as *I* and *me* and *who* and *whom* used correctly?
- ☐ Have you avoided sentence fragments and run-ons?
- ☐ Are commonly confused words such as *lie* and *lay* and *effect* and *affect* used correctly?
- ☐ Have you avoided using double negatives?
- ☐ Have you used active sentences, instead of passive ones, whenever possible?

Mechanics (punctuation and capitalization)

- ☐ Does every sentence begin with a capital letter?

Resources for Writers

Proofreading Checklist (cont.)

- ☐ Does every sentence end with an end mark (a period, question mark, or exclamation mark)?
- ☐ Are commas, semicolons, and other punctuation marks used correctly?
- ☐ Are all direct quotations enclosed in quotation marks or, in the case of quotations longer than three lines, set off and indented from either side?
- ☐ Do all proper nouns and proper adjectives, including the names of people and places, use initial capitals?

Spelling

- ☐ Are all words used in the paper spelled correctly?
- ☐ Have you checked the spellings of any names of people or places that you have used? ■

Glossary

abhor, *v.* To regard with horror or hatred, to detest

accord, *n.* Agreement, harmony

apostrophe, *n.* A literary device in which a nonhuman thing is addressed directly, as though it were a person

apprehension, *n.* Uneasy anticipation, dread

apt, *adj.* Quick to learn and understand

ardently, *adv.* Passionately, enthusiastically

barbarity, *n.* Lack of cultivation or familiarity with civilization, savagery

benevolence, *n.* The inclination to perform kind, charitable acts; such an act

blunt, *v.* To make less sharp, deaden

brook, *v.* Put up with, tolerate

calamity, *n.* An extraordinary disaster causing great loss or grief

chattel, *n.* An article of movable personal property, such as a cow or wagon

commensurate, *adj.* Corresponding in size or degree

comply, *v.* To act in accordance with another's command or request

concert, *n.* Communication of and agreement in actions or beliefs

conjecture, *n.* Guess or interpretation made by inference

consolation, *n.* Comfort

console, *v.* To comfort, to relieve of sorrow or grief

conspire, *v.* To plan secretly

contempt, *n.* A feeling that something or someone is inferior or worthless; scorn

cudgel, *n.* Short, heavy stick with a rounded end

cunning, *n.* Skill in deception, guile

defile, *v.* To pollute, make filthy

destitute, *adj.* Lacking necessary resources or possessions

defiance, *n.* Bold resistance, opposition to authority

digress, *v.* To turn aside from the main subject of a conversation or argument

Glossary

Vocabulary from the Text (cont.)

dilapidated, adj. Broken-down, shabby, having fallen into a state of disrepair

diligently, adv. Marked by steady effort

discord, n. Lack of agreement or harmony

dissipation, n. Wasteful spending or consumption

divest, v. To deprive or rid oneself of, as of rights or property

dregs, n. The bottom part of a liquid, containing sediment that has settled; the least desirable portion

ecstasy, n. Intense joy or delight

egotistical, adj. Conceited, self-centered, or boastful

eloquent, adj. Vividly or movingly expressive

emaciated, adj. Bony; very thin, especially from starvation

entreaty, n. Earnest request, plea

erroneous, adj. False, mistaken

esteem, v. To value greatly

evince, v. To show clearly

exculpate, v. To clear of guilt or blame

execrate, v. To denounce, to declare to be hateful

exhort, v. To urge by strong argument, advise

feasible, adj. Capable of being accomplished, possible

feeble, adj. Lacking strength, weak

fiendish, adj. Extremely wicked or cruel

fluent, adj. Able to express oneself effortlessly

forte, n. Something in which a person excels

fraud, n. A deception deliberately practiced to secure unfair or unlawful gain

fretful, adj. Marked by worry or distress

gallant, adj. Valiant or unflinching in action or battle

galling, adj. Causing extreme irritation

gory, adj. Bloody, wounded

grave, adj. Serious

harass, v. To irritate or torment persistently

Glossary

homage, n. The act of showing honor or respect

imbibe, v. To drink, to take in

imbue, v. To inspire or influence; to permeate or saturate

immutable, adj. Unchanging and unchangeable

impertinent, adj. Rude, inappropriate

impudence, n. Contempt for others or offensively bold behavior, disrespect

impudent, adj. Disrespectful

imputation, n. The act of attributing fault or responsibility to

incoherent, adj. Lacking connection or sense; said often of speech

indignation, n. Anger provoked by injustice or wrongdoing

indispensable, adj. Absolutely necessary; not to be done without or done away with

ineffable, adj. Incapable of being expressed or described

inevitable, adj. Unavoidable, sure to happen

infernal, adj. Suitable to or found in hell, wicked

insurrection, n. Open revolt against civil authority

intimation, n. Indirect communication, hint

jargon, n. Incoherent talk; also, the specialized language of a particular group

joist, n. A supporting timber in a floor or ceiling

lacerated, past part. Torn, mangled, or wounded

languish, v. To become weak or feeble; lose strength

lax, adj. Lacking in rigor, not strict

lingering, part. Slow in leaving, especially out of reluctance

loathe, v. To dislike greatly

lofty, adj. Of great height, elevated, exalted

maxim, n. A rule of conduct expressed as a saying or proverb

misdemeanor, n. A misdeed; a small offense, less serious than a felony

Glossary

obdurate, *adj.* Hardened in wrongdoing, stubborn

odiousness, *n.* Hatefulness

odium, *n.* A state of disgrace resulting from hateful conduct; strong dislike

pernicious, *adj.* Destructive

perpetrator, *n.* One responsible for carrying out an action, especially a crime

perplexing, *adj.* Confusing, puzzling

perseverance, *n.* Steady persistence, determination

piety, *n.* Religious devotion; the desire to perform religious duties

pretension, *n.* A doubtful claim

profligate, *adj.* Recklessly wasteful or extravagant

propriety, *n.* That which is proper or socially acceptable

providence, *n.* Care; divine direction and protection

prudence, *n.* Wisdom, exercise of good judgment

quail, *v.* To flinch, give way, or falter

rapturous, *adj.* Expressing overwhelming emotion

redress, *n.* Compensation for a wrong, loss, or injury

ridicule, *n.* Words or actions intended to evoke laughter toward another person

righteous, *n.* Morally upright

rigid, *adj.* Inflexible, unyielding

rude, *adj.* Lacking sophistication or refinement

sagacity, *n.* Soundness of judgment, wisdom

sanction, *n.* Authoritative permission or approval

scathing, *adj.* Harshly critical

servile, *adj.* In the manner of a servant, overly submissive

severe, *adj.* Causing great distress, harsh

shun, *v.* To purposefully avoid or keep away from

Glossary

singular, *adj.* Unusual or remarkable, unique

staid, *adj.* Serious, sober, marked by self-restraint

stratagem, *n.* Clever scheme for achieving an objective

stupor, *n.* A state of greatly decreased sensibility or physical activity

subversion, *n.* The act of undermining existing authority

supposition, *n.* An assumption, something supposed

suppress, *v.* To put down, especially by force

tranquil, *adj.* Composed, calm, free from anxiety

treacherous, *adj.* Dangerous, not to be relied on, not trustworthy

trifle, *v.* To waste

turbid, *adj.* Lacking clarity, foul, muddy

unabated, *adj.* Continued at full strength or force

urchin, *n.* Mischievous, playful youngster

unutterable, *adj.* Defying description or expression, beyond words

vestige, *n.* A visible trace, evidence, or sign of something that once existed

vindicate, *v.* To provide justification or support for

visaged, *adj.* Faced. From the noun *visage*, meaning "face."

wrath, *n.* Extreme anger

wretched, *adj.* Miserable, unhappy, distressed

yoked, *past part.* Joined with a harness